MOTHER CAME TOO

TONY SPENCER

Published by Tony Spencer
For further enquiries and additional copies
please contact: tonczere@btinternet.com

Printed by PML Ltd

CONTENTS

CHAPTER ONE

A MID-LIFE CRISIS

Having survived the trials and tribulations of life, marriage and developing a business career, I should have been able to settle down to a few years of "reaping the benefits". Then it hit me, THE MID-LIFE CRISIS. It dawned on me that there were another twenty years of work before I could hope to retire or, put another way, only twenty years before I became too old to enjoy "it", whatever "it" might be.

My business interests were sufficiently successful to enable me to sell up and have a look round for an adventure. I had read an article somewhere about life in Northern France which sounded very attractive, the only problem being that I needed to be able to earn a living there. Although I had done many different types of work in England, I could only think of one comparatively simple way that I could make a start.

Seven years earlier, I had enjoyed a one week holiday in Marbella and had been asked, by the owner of the villa, to deliver an envelope to an Englishman living in nearby Fuengirola. After a little searching, I found him playing tennis and, like me, enjoying the weather. I handed him the envelope and, naturally, asked him if he was having a good holiday.
"Oh no" he replied enthusiastically, "I live here."
"Really" I replied, "took early retirement did you?"
"No no" he said with a wry smile "I run my own business here looking after holiday homes for English owners and this envelope is payment for work I did for your villa owner. Very welcome it is too."

We enjoyed a coffee together and chatted a little about the pro's and con's of living and working in a "foreign" country and I set off to find a coach back to my friend's holiday villa. Needless to say, I fantasised somewhat about the possibilities of what looked like the ideal life. I completed my wonderful week's holiday and flew back to England feeling renewed and ready to go back to developing my latest business project.

One business followed another until I reached the point where I was running five small businesses at the same time so my Mother, who was 71 at that time, was less than amused when I started talking about Northern France. However, the decision was made so I hitched my caravan to the back of my Citroen van and set off to have a look around.
It had occurred to me that, if I could find somewhere to live in Brittany, I would have

1

time to settle in before the English "stampede" drifted Westwards and out of Normandy so I had arranged to meet up with an English estate agent in a village mid-way along the Northern coast of Brittany. As I approached the meeting point, I started to look around for a camp site where I could park the caravan for a few nights so that I could explore the area before being dragged around endless properties.

I soon found a camp site and turned down the lane as indicated. The lane got narrower and narrower before turning into a cart track barely wide enough for my caravan. Just as I was beginning to worry, I turned the corner into a most beautiful site on the side of a hill leading down to the beach so I looked around for someone to ask about my caravan. Then it struck me. The last time I had spoken French was on my only other visit to France some 12 years earlier!!

"Er...Bonjour Monsieur" was all I could think of. This inspired the facial expression which I was soon to become used to, it said "oh no another bloody Englishman!" Fortunately, the reply was, at least, polite.
"Bonjour Monsieur."
Then it was my turn again so I bungled my way into asking if he had space for my caravan for a few nights and was surprised and relieved to find that I hadn't forgotten the little French that I had learned at school. I was invited to position my caravan on one of the pretty little terraces cut into the hillside and then to pop into the bar for a glass of wine when I was ready. First hurdle successfully negotiated.

It didn't take me long to learn that the camp site owner had only opened up for the Summer season two days earlier which explained why he had a spare site for me. He then proceeded to show me around the site with its little shop where I bought more wine and something for breakfast. He then indicated a little pathway which would take me to "La Plage". Despite the fact that it was, by now, ten o'clock at night, it was still quite light so I took to the pathway to find out what a Plage was.

I had already discovered the exciting challenge of travelling alone in a "foreign" country and tasted the strange fear of how to make yourself understood but I was about to experience a new sensation. As I reached the end of the footpath, and was reminded that a Plage is a beach (loss of memory caused by excess of wine), my breath was taken away by the sheer beauty of the view which confronted me and I was suddenly conscious of the fact that there was no-one there with me to share the moment.
"Oh my God, look at that view" No-one answered and I cried with a mixture of elation and a kind of guilt that said "do I really deserve to be part of this"?

I wandered up and down the beach for an hour before I realised that it wasn't dark yet because it was the end of June and French time is one hour ahead of England. By the time I had found my way back to the caravan and finished the bottle of wine, I was almost convinced that this was the life for me. I was in a deep sleep before you could say "Ou est La Plage?"

I woke, next morning, not so bright and not so early but started to feel better after a shower and a couple of coffees so I secured my caravan and set off to meet my estate agent in the hopes that the caravan would still be there when I returned. My rendez-vous was at eleven o'clock in a village called Lezardrieux, just 15 miles from the camp site. The short drive took me along the coast with some stunning views of the cliffs and beaches on that part of the coast.

When I reached the centre of Lezardrieux, the old market square was lined on one side with half a dozen small shops, including the obligatory Bar and on the other side with several small office buildings, including the obligatory Mairie. Every commune has its Maire (Mayor) who, as I was soon to learn, seems to have the final say on most of what goes on in his commune. At one end of the square was the village church with graveyard, all of which was in immaculate condition despite being around 300 years old. There was a very narrow road by the side of the church which led down to the port and marina and then alongside the river to the point where it reached the English Channel.

The estate agent had asked me to meet her in the old market place and, of course, she had no trouble finding me since mine was the only English registered car in sight. She apologised for being 10 minutes late and suggested we had a coffee in the bar whilst looking through her folio to see how many properties might be of interest.
I was amazed to find so many houses for sale within my budget and, after some discussion, we selected three houses worth going to see.
"We can both travel in my car" she suggested "Leave yours here and I will bring you back later"
"Is it going to be safe left here?" I enquired, since one doesn't normally leave a car unattended in an English town for more than a couple of hours.
"Oh yes" she said with a smile "but I should take the keys out if I were you !!"
Was it really so safe here?

We had chosen to look at an old farmhouse which had been part renovated before the English owners ran out of money. Then there was a small house by the river which was the sort of house you see in oil paintings and finally a near derelict house about a mile from a village centre where there was a bar, a food shop, a magnificent church and the obligatory Mairie.

After looking carefully at all three, I told the estate agent that I would take a couple of days to think about it and see her on Friday with a decision.
I took a scenic route back to the caravan and was almost overwhelmed by the beauty of the area, it seemed as though every bend in the road revealed a new view of

beaches, rocky hills, dense but small forests and small villages. The Bretons take great pride in the cleanliness of their villages with most houses having well groomed gardens and the village centres lavishly decorated with small flowered areas carefully laid out to a theme often based on fairy tales. There were also lots of hanging baskets hanging on the lamp posts. This is a kind of civic pride that we seem to have lost sight of in England.

I was pleased to see that my caravan was intact when I arrived at the camp site because I was tired at the end of my busy day so I had a chat and a glass of wine with the camp site owner and enjoyed a light supper before curling up for the night.

The following day, I revisited the old farmhouse and had a good look around. It was in the middle of nowhere and, of the three buildings involved, each of them had some work done on them but none of them was finished or even remotely inhabitable and there was no land involved in the sale except for a small garden. I wondered if the vendors really had run out of money or if they had found insurmountable problems with each building and decided to abandon the project and hope to get their money back. By lunchtime, I had convinced myself that it was not worth the risk.I was also guided by my estate agent who had briefly explained about the French system for house purchase and had outlined some of the good points and some of the not so good ones. On the positive side, once you had made your offer and it was accepted, you went to the appointed Notaire, paid him a 10 per cent deposit and, along with the vendor, signed a Compromis. This effectively meant the deal was done and the only way you could get out of it without losing your deposit was if you needed a loan to buy and your loan was refused. Otherwise, both parties were committed to the sale at the agreed price and a completion date was mutually agreed. Job done.

On the down side, the house was sold on a WYSIWYG basis, in other words, what you see is what you get. The only report the vendor was obliged to submit was a very basic report on woodworm, termites and lead pollution. If you wanted anything structural to be checked, you had to pay for your own report. After completion, you had seven days to report any serious defects or other deceits. Job done.

On the drive back, I decided to stop for lunch in a small town near the coast called Treguier (Tregeeay). My agent, Jill, said that Wednesday was Market day and the town was worth a visit. This was an understatement. The market had virtually cleared by the time I arrived but there were still a few stalls left in the old Market Square which was in front of a very splendid Cathedral around which the town had obviously developed.

The town of Treguier had been a merchants port with shops lining the Market Square built in the timber framed style of the 15th century and later. The shops had a first floor overhang creating a sheltered parade over the shop windows. This architectural style makes the buildings look as though a strong wind would blow them over and there are hardly any properly vertical walls nor horizontal floors. I had never before looked at architecture in this way, but was profoundly impressed by the splendour of such a mosaic of odd shaped and sized buildings all perfectly clean and properly painted.

The streets leading away from the square were lined with shops and houses broken only by an occasional gap with a magnificent stone merchant's house set back from the street to allow for horse and carriage access and protected from the public by a tall railing fence and decorative iron gates.

I sat at a table in front of one of the many bars and restaurants in the square and enjoyed coffee and a sandwich as I watched the last of the stall holders packing up their stalls. My head was filling with unanswered questions such as why were there so many enormous churches and how on earth did they get those colossal stones up onto that spire without cranes, why were so many bars, open all day, and yet so few drunks and why did almost everyone I saw smile and say "Bonjour"?

I needed a chance to find the answers for myself.

As I drove along the coast road back towards the camp site, I decided to take another look at the abandoned house on the edge of the village. My idea was that there were bound to be aspects of the house which I had missed on my initial visit and all that I could remember of this house was that it was half buried in a sea of bramble and ivy and that it was on a dangerous bend on a busy road.

It was half a mile from the village of Quemper Guezennec and just a couple of miles north of the beautiful little town of Pontrieux. I had been right about the dangerous bend but the road wasn't so busy in the afternoon so I drove onto the "forecourt" and parked up. I had brought my camera with me but left it in the van since the first house wasn't worth photographing. I had just enough space to open my van door without hitting what must have once been a pretty little rockery garden so I trod carefully to avoid the scattering of large stones which were hidden beneath the bed of bramble surrounding the house and the stone wall which protected it from the road.

The house itself was quite small with only two windows and a door on the front, there were no other windows or doors and the two windows had iron bars in front of them as a security measure.

I had been inside the house, the day before, and it was in a terrible state with only boarded walls providing a small entrance porch with what must have been a wash room opposite the entrance. On the left was a small room which had been the kitchen with a very sorry looking Aga type cooker and a stoneware sink. On the right was the lounge with a traditional Breton open fire that had been half brick surrounded to an extent that it now looked like a hole in the wall at the bottom of the chimney.

I decided to take a look around the outside of the house to see if I could identify any features hidden by the foliage. On the end of the house were two and a bit walls of what might once have been a workshop or cattle shed. No roof survived and there was a large V shaped hole in the back wall where it had started to collapse. As I stepped carefully into this space, my eye was caught by something laying in the grass…..I needed no second opinion to confirm that it was an adder!!! It was obviously sleeping in the afternoon sun so I withdrew slowly and went back to the van to get my camera. The click of the camera caused the adder to wake up with a start and it rushed off immediately towards the back wall of the ruin, needless to say I trod very carefully for the rest of my visit.

I looked up at the chimney end of the house and saw a hole in the wall above ceiling level which had clearly been intentionally created since the sides were straight and the bottom was level with the ceiling. Presumably, it was there to give access to the roof space since there were no stairs inside the house. Behind the house was a one acre field which belonged to the house but was planted with maize, presumably by a local farmer, beyond that the land descended quite steeply to a river valley and presented a magnificent view of the forest on the other side of the valley.
All this for £7,500 !!!

The importance of the busy road and the dodgy access became less significant. The main road connected Quemper Guezennec to Paimpol which is a little fishing port only 10 kilometres from the house, so I took the road down crossing the valley and had a little wander around Paimpol. Being a fishing port, Paimpol has its old market square but with a smaller church and a "Halle Des Poissons" where fresh fish is sold on market day. There is a fairly large marina with many private boats and yachts surrounded by a narrow road lined with restaurants, bars and a couple of hotels. I looked at some of the menus and promised myself that I would come back to sample the local speciality of "Fruits De Mer"

I felt a little brighter the next morning despite having dreamed about being bitten by an adder on a sunny afternoon in the middle of nowhere. I decided to have a look at the third house by the river, it was only two miles from yesterday's house and less than one mile from the "Ville Fleurie" of Pontrieux. The French word for bridge is Pont so it made sense that the river Trieux passed through the middle of Pontrieux and the stretch of river between the village and the house on offer had originally been an industrious stretch with a lime kiln on one bank and a line of moorings on the other. In more recent times, most of the original industry had disappeared and been replaced by a large, unsightly docking area where sea sand was delivered and processed by a medium sized factory into various products used, I was told, in cosmetics manufacture.

The house on offer was, indeed, the most picturesque of the three being situated amidst a row of cottages on a bend in the river so I took off my rose coloured spectacles and had a closer look. The house itself was in very good condition and immediately inhabitable and the road, which passed directly in front of the house, came to an abrupt end only 200 metres beyond the house. No worries then.

As I stepped back from the front door, I noticed two previously unmentioned aspects which explained why it was so cheap. The river bank was only 10 metres from the front door and, since it was a tidal river, I thought it would possibly be liable to flooding. Much more important was that there was no back garden but a 10 metre high cliff topped by a railway line !!

I had lunch in Pontrieux, had a wander around and fell in love. La Ville Fleurie is really very pretty with a cobble stone street over the bridge which joins the two parts of the village. What appears to be the newer part has several shops, a hotel, a restaurant, the Post Office and the Mairie with the main access road leading westwards and only 100 metres or so to an Intermarche supermarket. The narrow cobbled street over the bridge is lined with much older shops and is only wide enough for an occasional delivery lorry. The square on the other side is actually triangular and has, at its narrower end, a carved stone water source used for watering horses and fed by the springs coming out of the hills directly behind the old square. This square has a patisserie, boulangerie, two restaurants and a bank. There is also a very old timber framed building which was, originally, the Mairie and is now a tourist information centre. Sadly, one is never sure when it is going to be open so it is better to ask in the local bar which is also a newsagent and bookmaker.

There is an atmosphere about the village of Pontrieux which is best described as romantic, calming and yet inspiring and I found myself looking more closely at the buildings, the shops and the people. The Breton people in this area are mostly farmers and are short and thick set, I remember thinking that I would not want to be on "the wrong side" of one of these people. Time would prove me to be wrong and the love affair with Pontrieux began.

After lunch, I went back to the abandoned house at Quemper Guezennec and called in at the village bar to buy some cigarettes. At that time, cigarettes were one third of the price in England but were only sold in bars, nowhere else. The lady who owned the bar in Quemper Guezennec was very pleasant and was keen to chat in English having spent some time in America so I had an ally. She told me that the house I was looking at belonged to an elderly lady who lived on the family farm on the edge of the village and it had been empty over 20 years since the lady's husband died. I went up to the house again. It was in a group of 4 houses which was called Kerraoul and had evidently been a farm worker's cottage belonging to the main farmhouse across the road.
On my third visit to the house, I had a closer look at the field behind and wondered what I would do with it, perhaps my own version of "The Good Life". Then I looked up at the roof and noticed several missing slates at the level where there should have been a drainage gutter. I took note of the approximate area that was missing and started to list the other things that would need to be done to make it inhabitable. The

trouble was that I had convinced myself that this was the house for me so my list of needs was much shorter than it should have been. Nevertheless, I telephoned the estate agent that evening and asked her if we could make an offer and, perhaps, sign the Compromis tomorrow, my last day before going home.

We met outside the Notaire's office at 10.30 on the Friday morning and I was introduced to Madame Guillard who, thankfully, had accepted my offer of £7,500 so we went into the office of the Notaire and I was introduced to Maitre Martin. The Notaire was a very dignified looking gentleman who peered over the top of his spectacles and bid us a good morning in perfect French before explaining that he had been educated in an English University but had long since forgotten our beautiful language. That dealt with, we got down to business and were done and dusted in less than an hour.

We agreed to come back to sign the completion (Acte De Vente) in eight weeks which meant that the holiday rush would be over and the ferry fares would be back down to an almost affordable level…very civilised. Once outside his office, I thanked Madame Guillard and my estate agent and apologised for rushing off but I had to retrieve my caravan and try to get back to St.Malo before the ferry sailed off back to England. The rest of the day rushed by with me in a haze of excitement mixed with panic whilst trying to remember to drive on the right side of the road.

It wasn't until I had settled onto the ferry that I started to think about what I had done…. What had I done? What would Mother say? Then I started to think about how I would wind up my affairs in England and then there were the girls. I have two wonderful daughters but had not been properly close to them since the divorce and, I must confess, I hadn't spent much time discussing my ideas with them or thinking what effects, if any, my departure would have on their lives or their opinions of me. Some of these questions would be answered the next day, some of them would be answered over the next 20 years but that's life.

The next eight weeks were not unusually stressful as I had realised that I had no idea of how to renovate an old house so I decided to take it one step at a time and concentrate on securing the roof so that it wouldn't get any worse during the months before I would be able to move permanently to France. I started out by asking a local builder's merchant if he could supply me with slates like the sample which I had brought back with me.
" You're joking mate" He said, fighting back the laughter.
"Our smallest slates are three times the size of that, you'll need a slate cutter."

So he sold me the equivalent square footage of slates and a tool like an enormous pair of scissors. The next thing I would need was a portable scaffold tower but I decided against buying a roof ladder since it was too expensive and too long to fit on the roof of my van without hitting the caravan in tow.

Fortunately, I had no house to sell before moving so I just took my businesses, one at a time, and either sold them or closed them down with the exception of my courier business which I held on to since it provided me with a good income and the Citroen van, which was so useful, as well as giving me the flexibility when I needed time off to do work on the house in France.

By the end of the eight weeks, I had heard nothing from the Notaire or my estate agent and I was getting nervous. I had, however, been assured that everything was in order so I booked my ferry ticket. It was at this point that Mother dropped her little bombshell.
"Can I come with you?" She asked as though we were going shopping rather than going to France.
Some discussion followed but she was determined so I bought her a passport and a ferry ticket, neither of which she had held before. For a woman of seventy years, that took more courage than I will ever know.

By the time the van was loaded with slates, tools, scaffold tower and caravan, it was looking more stressed than I was so we drove slowly to Portsmouth and then, the following morning, to the Notaire's office in Pontrieux. The completion of the purchase was going smoothly until the Notaire pointed out that the Vendor had agreed with the Council that they could take a slice of my garden, including the stone wall, on the bend in the road to widen the road and make it safer. I just had to hope that there wouldn't be any more little surprises in store. WRONG!!!

Having signed and "done the deal", we went up to the house. It was the first time Mother had seen it, she was horrified, it was covered in ivy and the interior was full of rubbish with bits of carpet and fallen wallpaper on the floor covering numerous dead mice and other unidentified skeletons!

We parked the caravan in the "old ruin", as it became known, and I started to unload my van whilst Mother began pulling the ivy from the walls, along with the only piece of guttering over the door. At least the house looked better when you could see the doors and windows!

Amongst my collection of tools, I had a step ladder so I enlarged the hole in the ceiling and climbed into the roof space. More rubbish including an old set of grain scales and a few other farming implements which confirmed that the roof space had, indeed, been used for drying and storing grain. As I looked around the inside of the roof, I could see that most of the roof boards had rotted at the point where they met the wall so they would obviously have to be replaced and I could also see that the two galvanised roof light windows had rotted allowing rainwater to fall onto the ceiling,

thus causing the ceiling boards to rot.
What had I bought?

Mother didn't speak much all evening. In any case, at 71, she was very tired from her first ferry crossing and all the excitement of visiting a foreign country for the first time. We had dinner in the caravan and slept well. Fortunately, we were going home the next day so the fact that there was neither water nor electricity to the house, meant that we would only have to " make do" for one night in the caravan.
The next morning we had a couple of hours to tidy up in the house and started to burn some of the rubbish in the fireplace when there was a knock on the door.
"Hello, I'm Richard and my family and I live in the village"
"Come in" I replied.
"We have neither water nor electricity, I'm afraid so I can't offer you coffee and I already drank the last of the wine".
"I saw your English registered van outside, as I drove by. You didn't buy this did you?!"

We spent the next hour discussing my house then his house. Richard and his family ultimately became good friends and their experience of life in France and coping with the bureaucracy was a priceless help.

The drive back was much easier without the caravan, tools and slates although the antique grain scales rattled somewhat in the back of the van. We took the scenic route back to St.Malo so that Mother could look around a bit and, thankfully, enjoyed a smooth return ferry crossing.

Since my Father's untimely death, some thirteen years earlier, I had promised God and my conscience that I would "look after" Mother, after all this is the woman who taught me how to walk. I was, nevertheless, more than surprised when she announced that she would love to come and live with me in France, if that is what I decided to do!!

Over the next few weeks, I formulated my plan for the renovation of my house. This was going to involve several trips across the Channel so that I could earn some money in the meantime and take "long weekends" over in France making the house safe and inhabitable. This, I determined, would probably take a year and for the first trip, my brother-in-law offered to come over with my sister and their two sons to help replace the rotten roof boards.
We arrived with the timber and began by taking off all of the old slates and carefully stacking them so that we could re-fit them later on. I found a local roofing contractor and asked him for a "Devis" for re-fitting the old tiles and finishing off with the new ones. More bad news.
The contractor arrived and immediately condemned the old slates as being porous.
He offered to supply and fit new roof slates for just a little less that I had paid for the

house !!!A new plan was needed. At least I had managed to get a stand pipe installed so we had running water to the house, albeit outside. The next thing to organise was electricity.

Since it was unlikely that I would be able to return for a couple of months, we decided to put some tarpaulin sheets on the now naked roof in the hopes that the weather would be kind to us and the rain would not be too heavy. I was naturally nervous about the weather and watched every weather report, once back in England. Needless to say, it rained a lot that summer and autumn and since the house was on a hill top, it was windy too. Fortunately, my new friend, Richard, passed by the house on his way to and from work so he kept an eye on things and my concerns were eased by his favourable reports.

Chatting to friends in England about my slate problem soon came up with a friend of a friend who did roofing work and would come over with me to replace the slates for a very modest fee. So I booked the ferry and sold my horse to give me enough money to buy the slates and off we went.

We soon found a friendly builder's merchant and my roofing friend was given a crash course on how the French fitted slate roof tiles using hooks instead of nails. This, it must be said, is a far superior system to the traditional method enabling the two of us to get the job done in five days. Actually fitting the slates was very hard but monotonous work although it did not take as long as I had feared. That left us with a day and a half to do "the tourist bit" and to recover from a tiring few days.

The house was, at least, ready for the winter months and I only needed one more visit to cover the access hole to the loft area so, for the final trip, I took my nephew for company and we spent a long weekend tidying up and preparing for what I had determined would be our arrival proper.

During the following months, I had some leaflets printed which I sent to all of the estate agents I could find, who were selling properties in Brittany. I also sold my courier business and bought a rather tired but sturdy minibus so that I would be able to take our belongings and very basic furniture in not more than two trips.
The last of my tasks was to find out as much as I could about the wildlife, especially the adder which I had encountered earlier on. I went to Twycross Zoo and asked to see the Manageress of the Reptile House to explain my situation and ask for her advice.
"Is there anything I should do about the adder, please and what do I do if it bites me?"
"Panic." Her one word reply did not impress me nor fill me with confidence.
Perhaps this was a sign for the future.
I booked our ferry tickets for late August and Mother and I moved in. The adventure was about to begin.

CHAPTER TWO

The Move

The first two weeks were very difficult since it was not possible to sleep in the house but we could, at least, cook and eat inside and, since September was fairly warm, it was not too difficult to set up separate sleeping areas in the house so we moved in.

The next step was to find a way of getting running water into the kitchen and arranging for a supply of electricity. Those early weeks were difficult enough for me, how on earth my seventy two year old Mother coped, I can only imagine. .But cope she did and she never complained during those long Autumn evenings in front of an open fire with only candles and a battery radio for entertainment.

During the daytime, we worked hard to establish ourselves and slowly the house became a home. It was around this time that the last of my savings went on materials and furniture so we now had only Mother's pension to buy provisions but, fortunately, I had a bicycle so that I could cycle into Pontrieux twice a week to go to the local supermarket. At almost the same time, the Exchange Rate Mechanism collapsed so the pension was reduced to around sixty pounds per week and that left only three pounds per week for petrol. To make matters more difficult, I had received no response from my leaflet mailing so there were no work prospects on the horizon.

Then, one morning, the men from the D.D.E. (environmental department) arrived with a digger, a lorry and two young men with traffic controlling Stop and Go signs. They had come to widen the road on the bend in front of my house. As soon as they started to demolish my front "garden", I realised that we were going to be somewhat exposed to the traffic so I asked them if they would put the stone, from the stone wall, on the field behind the house. I had no idea what I would do with it but, at least, I would have a choice. By the end of the day, the garden had gone and the bend was now six feet wider so I supposed that they would come back in a few days and put down some tarmac. They never did.

With the front of the house now exposed to the road, and the lorries going much faster round the bend, it was obvious that I would have to teach myself how to build a dry stone wall. That is one of those funny things in life where you have seen it being done on the television and thought to yourself "I bet I could do that" so I made a plan and got started.

Unfortunately, I only had a pickaxe and a wheelbarrow and some of the stones I

needed for the base of the wall weighed around one hundred kilo's. It took as much as two hours to roll them round from the field !!
After two weeks of back breaking work, I completed my first ever dry stone wall much to the amusement of the " regular" passers by. The most satisfying part is that, after almost 20 years, it is still standing!

By now, we were moving towards winter and I still had no prospect of work although mother and I were beginning to get the house in order and we now had a small garden in front of the house thanks mainly to our friends Richard, Jane and Richard's mother. During our many discussions with Richard and Jane, it had been suggested that, as soon as the farmer cleared his crop from my field, we should try the "Good Life" approach and plant some potatoes. Seed potatoes were very cheap so I prepared a corner of the field and gave it a try hoping for some sort of crop before Christmas.

I had also become friends with a local butcher who was also one of only 2 registered horse traders in the area. Dominique was, indeed, a good friend and asked if he could put a couple of his horses in my field in exchange for a steady supply of very cheap meat from his shop. So he turned up, one day, with a trailer loaded with fence posts and a couple of reels of electric fencing wire and, by the end of the day, we were ready for the first horses. Fortunately, I had my own electric transformer so the electric fence was turned on and the horses were introduced to the field and to mother and me. Having enjoyed a few years with horses in England, it was good to have someone to talk to who didn't answer back! Although there might have been times when a second opinion would have been helpful because I was about to tackle my next major new project.

Since there were no stairs inside the house, I needed to install a staircase and had been lucky enough to buy one from a friend in England. It was a very small and tight spiral staircase which had been an external fire escape for a demolished school near to my last home in England but was ideal for my house since we didn't have much spare room. Fitting the staircase is a bit like building dry stone walls really, you've seen it done on the television and it looks easy……. WRONG AGAIN! It took Richard and me three days to fit the staircase including making a hole in the ceiling to enable access into the roof space and the only area where we could fit it was in the old "bathroom" so this meant that I would have to improvise somewhat and create a bathroom in the empty roof space. Fortunately, mother was just able to negotiate the spiral stairs but we were still having to use a portable camping toilet which made emptying it a very unpleasant task.

One of my last acquisitions before leaving England had been to exchange my French grain scales for a very second hand shower cubicle, sink and toilet so my next new project would be to learn how to create and install a bathroom. The learning curve was beginning to steepen!

It was about this time that Richard introduced us to a builder called Bob (honestly). This kind and gentle giant turned out to be my saving grace in many ways. The initial introduction was to help me with my bathroom, actually fitting the sink, shower and toilet was the easy part, it was the plumbing which caused the difficulty but to Bob it was no problem, Until, that is, we came to fitting the toilet..... where would the " waste products" go? Apparently, there was no town sewage so I needed a septic tank (fosse septique) and, the way Bob described it, it was not going to be too difficult once I had bought a tank and buried it in the field that is!!!!!

I had just enough money to buy the smallest tank available and the builders merchant very kindly suggested that, if I dug the hole for the tank, they could deliver it and put it into the hole for me, the bad news was that the hole needed to be just over 2 metres by 2 metres and 2 _ metres deep. It took 12 days to dig the hole with only the pick axe, shovel and wheel barrow!!

During this time a large toad fell into the hole one night and didn't so much as thank me when I lifted him (or her) out! Then there was the time when the chickens escaped from the chicken run and, as I was trying to herd them back into their home, one of the chickens fell into the hole followed by a cloud of feathers and a loud chorus of screeching, as only a chicken can when it falls into a large hole in the ground which hadn't been there the week before!

Eventually, the hole was ready and the tank was delivered and lowered into place. The plumbing was completed and, miracle of miracles, we had a proper flushing toilet and a working sink and shower, all before Christmas! Life was beginning to become civilised for mother and me now that we had the basic necessities of life, even though they were somewhat basic.

Christmas day arrived and the weather was beautiful so we took a walk down to the village where the bar was open and, in compliance with French law, fresh bread was available so we bought some bits and bobs and walked home to enjoy a salad on our picnic table in the front garden. This must be the life we had been created for, we had an income without having to struggle by on mothers pension.

CHAPTER THREE

The Real Work Begins

Only three days later, we were tidying up in the front garden when a car pulled up in front of the house and a middle aged lady climbed out and asked, in very broken French spoken with a Scottish accent, if I could direct them to Mr Spencer's home. My prayers were answered!

The lady and her husband had bought a house in a nearby village through the estate agent I had used and had been advised to contact me with a view to looking after their house when they were at home in Canada. We chatted over coffee and mother and I were invited to visit their new house the next day since they were meeting the present owner to discuss the completion date in February.

The next morning, mother and I set off to find the little village of Troguery which was near to my favourite town of Treguier . The couple we had met the previous day were already at the house so we knocked on the door and were greeted by a very elegant lady who invited us in having been advised of our pending arrival.

The house was very small having only a lounge and modest kitchen downstairs with a bathroom off, upstairs were two bedrooms. Outside was a small but well manicured garden part of which was taken up by a conservatory leading to the kitchen. Explanations followed introductions and we soon found ourselves being offered more work once the sale of the house was completed since Margaret, the owner of the house, was moving into a larger house in the next village and she had plans to change the layout of the house as well as create a better garden. This was the beginning of a series of events which I could only have dreamed of and which would secure the future of my French adventure.

Just as mother and I were about to leave, Margaret's estate agent arrived and we were invited to join her for a coffee in the village bar the next day. Margaret's agent, Anna, was probably only a little older than me and was obviously very glamorous as a young woman.

One could easily imagine that she had seen and enjoyed many adventures and this was reflected in her warm and friendly manner. Meeting Anna was one of the most important events for me and would teach me about the art of "networking".

As I had hoped, there were several English families already in the area and a steady flow of people looking to buy properties, some to live in, and others hoping to rent our the houses as holiday homes known as "gites" and Anna's work meant that she was constantly meeting these people The French Government had created the Gite industry by encouraging farmers to renovate disused worker's cottages, with the help of a grant, and renting them out as holiday homes. This business grew quite rapidly so that "foreign" owners were soon buying these cottages and renovating them, without the help of a grant, and providing themselves with a real investment which might one day provide them with a modest pension.

So, now I had prospects for the future since Bob was already doing work for Anna's clients. Initially I was simply labouring for Bob and one of the first labouring jobs introduced me to a family who became very good friends whilst another labouring job introduced me to a lady who I would describe as exciting. I went to help Bob to do some work at a local manor house belonging to a lady called Lolita.

Lolita was another retired lady, living alone in an enormous and very splendid house with a separate cottage attached to it and Bob was in the process of converting it into a Gite. There were several other out-buildings but they were some what dilapidated and unlikely to be convertible, or so I thought. I was later to be proven wrong. The house was surrounded by a very large and beautiful garden of around two acres and Lolita was devoted to developing and maintaining the garden so, for a retired lady, she was always very busy and extremely fit.

Since Lolita was of a similar age to my mother, they quickly became friends and mother had a "target" to help maintain her own fitness. The house also had its own private chapel nearby which Lolita used to encourage her friends, English and French, to meet up on suitable religious occasions. The Breton people are always very aware of their religion so the locals enjoyed Lolita's little "events", which usually ended up with tea and biscuits or something a little stronger, and gave we English an opportunity to integrate. I was, therefore, pleased, relieved and grateful that, just as I was beginning to worry about finding work and company for mother, things began to happen.
Early work with Bob quickly showed me how little I knew about maintenance and renovation word so the learning curve became even steeper, thank goodness Bob was so patient with me.

I did, however, enjoy one particular advantage since Bob spoke no French, not a word, and I had discovered a natural ability with the language so my lessons in building work were repaid by my new found translation skills although I did struggle a little with the more technical terms which caused some strange comments from the builders merchants.

As my finances improved, I was able to make better progress on my own house and I was now able to afford new wood and nails instead of recycling old ones so I was able to create bedrooms upstairs and create a much better kitchen downstairs. So far as my field was concerned, we ate the chickens and decided not to bother with any more since they cost us £7 each including feed and the potatoes were ruined by blight so my horse trading friend Dominique suggested I try a couple of goats and sheep. This seemed like a good idea since neither required special care and both would keep the grass short. The sheep were supplied by Dominique and he had a friend who wanted to sell a female goat, the idea being that we should mate it with a local farmers buck and we would then have a kid to eat and goat's milk to follow.

The animals were delivered and the sheep instantly devoted itself to running away from us. The goat, on the other hand, was quite friendly if a little "playful" and would enjoy an occasional sparring session with me before enjoying a chunk of two day old bread offered as a reward. As the weeks went by, the goat became more of a friend whilst the sheep continued to avoid me. Then the day came to take the goat off to be mated and, after some effort from mother and me, we loaded her into the back of the mini bus and drove to a nearby farm where she was introduced to a rather smelly and dominant male.

Judging by her response to his advances, I began to wonder if I had bought the worlds first lesbian goat, a suspicion which was confirmed when, after several weeks, Dominique declared that she was not pregnant and so would be returned to the farmer who had sold her to us. In the meantime, I had met an English lady who was breeding goats and had two male kids which she wanted to sell so I took them home and introduced them to the sheep. During the weeks to follow, I got into the practice of taking them for walks, on a lead, down the lanes and the goats and I became good friends. This was not one of my better ideas.

CHAPTER FOUR

My Business Begins

By the time February came, work was improving nicely and I had begun to get a little early gardening work at the house in Trougery, also the lady who sold the Trougery house, had moved into her latest acquisition and Bob had started to open out the ground floor to create a kitchen/diner. The front door of the house opened directly onto the street, there being no pavement, and there was no access to the rear garden so everything had to be carried through the house whilst the rear garden had a small brook running down one side and across the bottom with the neighbour's garden on the other side, the whole garden being surrounded by a brick wall. Built on to the back of the house was a very basic conservatory that had a waist high brick wall topped by a very crudely constructed glazed wall and a corrugated clear plastic roof. This conservatory was perfectly functional and offered a pleasant lunch room until the sun shone when it became a torturously hot sauna!

The main work inside the house was completed by early summer by which time attention had turned to the garden and to painting the outside conservatory and other windows. There were a couple of brick built outbuildings down the brook side of the garden with a small slabbed area at the bottom where Bob decided to create what he called a gazebo. This done, he moved on leaving me to deal with the garden. There were several well established bushes in the border on the opposite side of the garden to the sheds, a small fig tree in the corner by the gazebo and a small lawn in the centre. The only other plants of interest which I could find were three abandoned grape vines buried under the bramble and weeds at the base of the conservatory end wall. After much discussion about the future of the conservatory, the owner finally relented and agreed to allow me to clean up the vines and pass them through a hole in the conservatory wall in the hope that they could be trained to grow inside the roof and thus provide a natural leafy blind to reduce the heat of the sun. The plan worked like a miracle and by the second summer there were bunches of grapes to be had as a bonus.

By the end of the summer, Dominique announced that it was time to "deal" with my sheep and goats and we arranged that he would slaughter and butcher them for me in exchange for half of the sheep meat. This sounded quite straight forward until he arrived at my house with his tool kit and announced that "of course" we would deal with them on my premises so that I could help him!!

Killing the sheep, called Barbara, was not too difficult since one carefully positioned

stab with an appropriately sharp knife ensured that the sheep died instantly and without any pain. Then it was the turn of the two goats. When I went into the field to collect them, they thought it was time for walkies and trotted enthusiastically towards me, at which time I froze. How on earth was I going to deal with this? I fought off the tears and grappled with my conscience as Dominique had told me to hold them until they stopped moving whilst he cut their throats!
Of all of the good, bad, easy and difficult things I did during my time in France, nothing ever matched the emotions I experienced in those few short but very long minutes.

Once the animals were dead, dealing with them became easier and Dominique and I took them into my workshop and suspended them from the roof beams so that they could hang and drain for 24 hours when he would come back to butcher them. I went to work, the next day, at Lolita's manor house and she immediately noticed my lowered spirits and asked what was wrong. She suggested that I should ask Dominique to skin the animals so that I could take the skins to a nearby tannery and have them treated to enable me to keep the skins as a souvenir.

Visiting the tannery was something of a surprise, although I had no idea what to expect, since they had a reception room with shop where you could buy treated skins, I was taken on a guided tour of their works to see for myself what they did. The only part of the tour which I remember is the incredible smell and the sight of so many sheep and cattle skins in various stages of treatment. I was asked to return in two weeks to collect my souvenirs by which time the meat had been skilfully butchered by Dominique and was put into my freezer minus his half of the sheep. I have to admit that, although the slaughtering episode was a gruesome affair, the meat was delicious, especially the goats, and the skins provided us with very luxurious bedside mats so their memory lived on for some years.

As the school holidays began, the tourists started to arrive so I soon picked up a couple of clients who paid me to clean their gites, meet and greet their visitors and clean up when they left. This was the business I wanted most of all since the cleaning was not nearly so hard as labouring for Bob the builder and most of the visitors were interesting people although some of the exceptions made me ashamed to be English.

Later on, that summer, my friend Richards's wife, introduced me to an owner who had four gites together and was running a successful business letting them out for the summer so my gite cleaning enterprise immediately doubled in size and I was thankful that mother was only too keen to help out.

The "block of four", as it came to be known, became an important part of my enterprise after the second summer when the owner sold his property to two new owners whose first project was to install a swimming pool. One of the partners was an English builder so he did the work himself with the help of his "right hand man" in England so no work for me which was not too disappointing after he told me that he had served his apprenticeship with that well known Cornish building company Bodgitt & Scarper!! They had been advised to get a local contractor to bring his digging machine to re arrange the front garden for the pool. This was my introduction to the world of Sven, a colourful German character who lived in the village next to the gites. He had bought an old farm house with out buildings and was in the process of renovating the whole to create a house for himself with a second house for his parents to live in upon their pending retirement. This on the outskirts of a village called Pommerit Le Vicomte.

Despite the fact that the village was "in the middle of nowhere" Pommerit was a beautiful village maintained and cared for by the commune lead by its mairie, as always. There was a triangular market square skirted by a couple of shops, a post office, a veterinary practice and the obligatory two bars. At one end of the square was a small but very useful supermarket and, just a hundred yards down the road, a boulangerie and a magnificent church. Next to the church was a hotel restaurant with bar and a fourth bar another hundred yards further along. The block of four gites was just half a mile from Pommerit in a very secluded group of farm houses which made it very popular with the English tourists. And, during my third year in France, Pommerit would become very important both to my work and my social life.

Meeting Sven with the digger was a great help when it came to house renovations since most of the properties we worked on needed either landscaping work or septic tanks fitted, the benefits worked both ways since Sven didn't do building work so we were able to exchange contacts.

As my work load increased, so did my revenue and since my minibus needed repairing and, being English registered, was not really suitable I decided to take advantage of my houses's position on a comparatively busy road and put a sign in the window offering it for sale "a vendre". Before too long we had a couple of enquiries then, one day, a surprise. There was a knock on the door and I opened the door to me greeted by a pleasant traveller and, parked rather dangerously on the bend in front of the house, an ancient Massey Ferguson tractor with a gypsy roulotte in tow!!
His first words reminded me of my arrival at the campsite at the beginning of my adventure
"er bonjour monsieur" a dead giveaway, another Englishman.
"Hello" I said "how can I help you"
" I have come about the minibus" he seemed relieved.
I fetched the keys and opened the doors, started the engine and a sale was agreed in a matter on minutes. I then asked him about his mobile home so he invited Mother and me to have a look.
Following my comment on his "mobile home", mother and I were invited to have a

look inside where we met his girlfriend who had been looking after their dog. The roulotte was a beautifully restored original which had been fitted with car wheels and, internally, with a more modern sink and cooker. He introduced himself and his girlfriend and explained that she was Dutch and that her father restored and sold these old gypsy caravans at home in Holland. They spent their winters in Holland then drove over to Brittany, with the tractor, so that they could earn a living on the summer markets with Paul playing his guitar and singing and Moira making and selling small leather goods such as purses and wristbands. They were interested in buying my mini bus so that they could travel more easily and thus find a more permanent site for the tractor and caravan.

A deal was agreed and we waved goodbye to our mini bus. The next time we saw Paul, he had bought a small house near Callac and was planning to "settle down" in Brittany.

Having raised a little cash on the sale of the mini bus, I contacted a young man who had enquired about the mini bus and claimed to do a little buying and selling. It made sense to buy a left hand drive car and William had offered me an early Renault 5, which was in good condition for only £600. he came to my house with the car and I explained to him that I only had £500 from the mini bus. Imagine my surprise when he said that I could have the car now and pay him the balance when I could! We shook hands on the deal and he explained that, in Brittany, a deal is done on a handshake and you are trusted to honour the agreement there by.

Mother and I were invited to take the balance of the sale to William's home and were impressed to see that he lived in the keepers lodge on his uncle's estate near Paimpol and enjoyed beautiful views of the cluster of small islands just out to the sea. We were introduced to his wife, who was expecting their first child, and offered coffee according to custom. Our good fortune, in meeting William, continued when he told us that his uncle lets him stay in the lodge in exchange for keeping the estate in order and keeping the many trees properly maintained and he could sell the logs to subsidise his income. This was a real bonus for us since we were going to need some heating for the winter which was likely to be cold for us in our little house on the hilltop.

Now that we had a cheap little car, I could take mother to some of the social events to which we had been invited, these were mainly barbeques or dinners at the homes of the ever growing English population in our region. It never ceased to amaze me how many of these people either wanted "little" jobs done or knew someone who had just bought a home and wanted it renovated or, at least, modified. In this way, Bob the builder, Sven the digger man and I were soon able to find full time work.

One of the many couples we met in those early days was a husband and wife who had a very nicely restored farmhouse near to my favourite town of Treguier, I had worked with Bob on some of the renovation work there and enjoyed their hospitality on several social evenings. It was during these conversations that mother and I were reminded of the importance of what my father had always described as "not closing the doors behind you when you leave", this way you can always go back.

During my motor cycle "career", one of my friends in the paddock and enemies on the track had a beautiful girlfriend and made off with another girl. Since they lived in nearby Derby, I took advantage of the situation and enjoyed some weeks in the company of his girlfriend. Unfortunately for me, my friend decided that his regular girlfriend was better than he thought and proposed marriage which she accepted. An extraordinary coincidence then that I should be doing work in France for the girl he had "dumped" all those years ago! Needless to say, many happy memories were relived over dinner that evening and I was both pleased and relieved that her current husband joined in with the reminiscences.

During our first summer in France, my oldest daughter Philippa came to visit us, for three days, with an old school friend but both girls were very tired and spent most of their time with us sleeping. It must be said, though, that the Breton air was so much "fresher and cleaner" that it took a few days to get used to and the immediate effect was to make one sleepy.

The following summer, my youngest daughter, Vikki, came to stay for a couple of weeks and, during that stay, met Anne, the girl from Derby. Despite their age difference, they immediately became friends and Anne was delighted that Vikki was a very capable horse rider so that they could go horse riding together and explore the beautiful country side surrounding their house.

At the end of that summer, Anne and her husband Pen decided it was time to move on and they felt that a move to the south of France was a good idea so they bought a farm which had been a goat breeding farm until it was bankrupted. Under French law, under such circumstances, a property is offered for sale by auction and the reserve price is the value of the debt to be recovered so, provided you can pay on the day, there are some extraordinary bargains and Pen and Anne's farm was indeed a bargain. I went, with Pen, on new years day to help them move in and took mother, in our recently acquired Renault 5, to stay for a few days in the following spring.

The farm had over 60 acres of land with it so Anne's horses were more than happy in their new environment. On the down side, however, it was an eight hour drive and, by the time we got back, my poor little car had a nervous breakdown and refused to do any more work until I replaced the water pump and alternator!!

Back at home, our little house was progressing nicely and my gite cleaning work, by this time involving eight gites, was keeping us well fed especially since they all needed their gardens to be serviced. Also, the "block of four" gites at Pommerit Le Vicomte now had its swimming pool working so I added pool servicing to my growing list of services.

After my experiences with potatoes, chickens, sheep and goats, my friend Dominique suggested to me that I may consider buying a pony and, by coincidence, he knew of a "lovely little youngster" that a friend of his had to sell. Having had good experiences with horses in the past, I agreed to go with him to see what was on offer. We arrived at his friend's farm and were shown into a barn where the horse had been put for my inspection. She was a pretty Connemara pony of around thirteen hands height and, I was told, sixteen months, too small and too young to be anything other than a companion to help to keep the grass down in my field. Matters were not helped when I picked up one of her front feet to check the condition of her hooves...... she fell over!!! Apparently, French horses were not used to having their feet looked at especially since this particular pony had lived in a field since birth and had not been so much as groomed by a human. But since she was very pretty and the asking price was more than reasonable so, I thought, given eighteen months of care and training, I might be able to sell her on and make a profit. A price was agreed and we shook hands on the deal, Dominique came to my field the next day and helped me create a small paddock, with my electric fence, and we quickly erected a simple "lean to" shelter at the back of the house where she could sleep.

Two days later, Dominique arrived with the pony in his trailer and advised me that it is normal, in France, to name a horse according to its month of birth so, since mine was born in May, her name should begin with an E. I talked with Mother about it and she could only think of Emily so my new pony was named Emily, Emmy for short, and our relationship was founded. Emmy only escaped from my field twice before she realised what electric fencing was about and that the passing lorries have very loud horns which they blast at you if you try to play on the road. Once that adjustment had been made to her thinking, we settled down and I was able to begin her training by first teaching her that we could communicate without necessarily using words. Because I had plenty of grass in the field, I only needed to boost her diet with occasional apples, carrots and the odd left over scraps from the kitchen plus, of course the obligatory garlic. The first time Dominique saw me giving garlic to Emmy, he was puzzled, to say the least, and asked what on earth I was doing. When I explained that it was an old gypsy practice for helping keep the flies away from the horse and to aid its breathing, he began to take notice after that and, when he next came to sell one of his horses, which was in my field, I over heard him telling the buyer about an English "trick" he had learned for keeping the flies away from the horse!!

I had no trouble in bonding with Emmy as she was a very affectionate horse and enjoyed our time together especially when I started taking her for walks on a lead rope. It was on one of these walks when a series of events caused me to meet a villager called Guy. I had only just set off down a bridle path opposite my house when a passing lorry hit a hollow in the road making a very loud bang which startled both the horse and me. She immediately set off in panic and I was dragged, face down, to the floor before letting go of her lead rope. I was bleeding quite badly from the various wounds I had suffered and had no choice but to go home and clean up, by which time there was no sign of Emmy so I could only wander off in the direction she was last seen in the hopes of finding her. After an hour of searching, I gave up and went back home to see if she had turned up but no such luck. Another hour passed by and I was just about to set off for another look when there was a knock on the door and there stood a boy, of around twelve years of age, holding Emmy!!!

"c'est votre cheval, je crois monsieur"

He introduced himself as Gael and, by the time I had shaken him by the hand and claimed my horse back, he was joined by a man of around forty years who introduced himself as Guy and explained that they had found Emmy grazing quietly in a lane about two miles away and that he recognised her as living in my field.

It is not difficult to imagine my relief and gratitude so, as soon as Emmy was back in the field, I invited Guy and Gael into the house for a glass of wine and a chat which lasted over half an hour whilst we exchanged observations on my progress on the house and I introduced Mother having then to translate back and forth, which was, at least, good practice for my French language skills. Since the horse had suffered no damage and I ended up with only one scar, it could be said that our little "unplanned" adventure had helped with more French friends since Guy had invited us to visit his home and looked forward to meeting my youngest daughter, Vikki, who was due to join us for her summer school holiday. I had hoped that Vikki, who was already capable and enthusiastic with horses, would be able to help me in training Emmy but, unfortunately by now, Emmy had decided to be a "one man horse" and Vikki and Emmy took an instant dislike to each other. Still, once the initial feelings had been overcome, Vikki was indeed a great help and soon introduced Emmy to the benefits of exercising on a lunge rein.

My friends Jack and Mary had two children, a son known as little Jack, and a daughter Anne Marie who was a similar age to Vikki so they quickly bonded and enjoyed numerous excursions together exploring the area and looking for boys but with only modest success.

My new friend Guy was delighted to meet Vikki and introduced her to his wife and two young children and, being typically generous and outgoing, invited us to join him on his motor boat for a day out on the river. We met at his mooring in Pontrieux in the morning, as soon as the rising tide permitted, set off with Vikki and Anne Marie, accompanied by suitable good looking young men, Guy and myself. We motored off downstream, past the Chateau De La Roche Jagu and out towards Lezardrieux. This was the village where I had originally met my estate agent. The estuary soon began to widen as we passed Lezardrieux and we were looking out onto the English channel. I wasn't over confident with Guy's piloting skills since he was continually going off course as he let go of the steering wheel to roll another cigarette! He reassured me by telling me he was actually avoiding the shallow water and then proceeded to invite me to guide the boat whilst he refilled his tobacco tin! As we headed towards the open sea, Guy pointed out that the Isle De Brehat was only a short distance off shore and suggested that, since it was such a lovely, calm day, we should go there to have a look around. We reached the island before lunch and moored up in a very pretty and private little bay, the inflatable dingy was unloaded and we rowed, Robinson Crusoe style, ashore.

The water, in the bay, was crystal clear so we enjoyed a brief swim in the sea, a first for me, before having our sandwiches and a glass or two of wine. The island itself is very small so only the doctor is allowed a car and the only tractor, on the island, doubled up as a guided tour vehicle once the trailer was hitched up. It made more sense to walk round so that we were able to enjoy the little craft shops and visit a glass blowing workshop. By late afternoon, Guy suggested that we should go back so that we could catch the incoming tide and be home before dark. It didn't quite work out as we caught up with the tide and had to moor up at the Chateau De La Roche Jagu whilst we waited for the tide to catch up with us. We "foreigners" were amazed to stand on the shore and literally watch the tide coming in as it rose by around six meters twice a day. We arrived back at Pontrieux just before dark and thanked our host for a marvellous day out before returning to our respective homes to finish the red wine and sleep well into the next day. Work, that summer, was beginning to pick up and I was grateful to have both mother and Vikki to help with the cleaning as several of my gites were some miles apart so I could leave mother and Vikki to prepare the block of four gites whilst I chased around doing the others.

It was around this time that I was introduced to a very pleasant lady who lived in the nearby village of Pommerit Jaudy. She was a retired lady who had settled in the area, some years earlier, to be near to her daughter who was finishing her education in France and had become acquainted with a wealthy French building contractor who had a holiday home in my favourite town of Treguier.
He had recently bought a ruined windmill and set about renovating it so I was asked to do some finishing touches inside the windmill and then to begin clearing the surrounding land so that a garden could be created. The building itself was only five metres diameter and had been restored with no expense spared. On the ground floor was the kitchen and bathroom with a bedroom on the first floor. The top of the mill had been ruined many years earlier so the owner, being a builder, had created a small but quite spectacular lounge in timber with a 360 degree glazed viewing area. The views were stunning with one side of the mill looking over the rocky cliffs and, past some small uninhabited islands, out to sea. The views inland were equally beautiful looking across country to the nearest small village. The electrical system, including

central heating, was designed in such a way as to enable the owner to telephone the mill from his home in Paris and control the heating, lighting, etc by remote.

The surrounding land, however, was completely wild being mostly covered by a six feet high web of bramble and weeds. The only equipment I had, at that time, capable of dealing with the bramble was an electrical hedge trimmer so it took many hours of extremely hard work to clear with me cutting it down and Mother, with a rake, dragging it into heaps so that we could burn it as appropriate. We were most relieved when that job came to an end although we did, at least, earn enough money to buy a petrol engined strimmer so the next garden creating jobs were much easier.

Having completed that work, I was asked to do some small jobs in his main holiday house in Treguier and this proved to be an important part in my building and renovation education. The house was situated on a narrow street which lead from the main cathedral square in Treguier, a street which comprised mainly of shops and medium sized houses which looked as though they might once have been the homes of book keepers and middle management people. Half way up the street was a very splendid merchant's house which stood back from the street and was fronted by iron railings and double gates, obviously intended to give carriage access. Three of the houses had been converted into restaurants and only a couple of houses, including my client's house, were as originally intended.

Most of the properties on the street looked to be two hundred years old or more and there were a couple of very old ones with the upper floors made in the timber framed, wattle and daub style. The house I was to work on was one of these old buildings and I was immediately enthralled to see the timber beams inside, some of which had scars of earlier joints suggesting that they might have served another purpose in a previous life. None of the earlier timber showed signs of being machine cut although most of them had suffered wood worm, at some stage, which had obviously been long since treated. The main beams inside were up to one foot square in section and not particularly straight and yet one was never in doubt as to their strength. The work I was to do was in an extension which had been built on to the back of the house to make a bathroom and extra bedroom, the whole having been completed long before planning permission and design safety was imposed. Nevertheless, I enjoyed the privilege of working inside a property of such antique splendour and, since my work needed no changes to the main fabric of the building, I was able to enjoy learning about its construction and observing the methods that must have been used to build and later develop it.

CHAPTER FIVE

The Learning Curve

My apprenticeship with Bob the builder was progressing very well, at this point, covering some very interesting work renovating older properties. One such was the "reclamation" of an old farm house which had obviously started its life on the edge of the village of Plouec Du Trieux, only a couple of miles from Pontrieux. The land surrounding the farm had long since been sold off and built upon and the original outbuildings abandoned. It took mother, with her rake and wheelbarrow, and me with my heavy duty strimmer, a couple of days to cut back the brambles and gain access to the buildings.

The farm consisted of a small bungalow style cottage with a forge and workshop built on the side of it. Beyond that was what looked like a small single room accommodation. The three units were joined by a common roof space which ran the whole length of around fifty or sixty feet. Built off of the back of the small single room unit and forming an L shape, was the old animal shed or pig sty.
The owner had determined to recover each of the buildings in phases starting with the original farmhouse which, once the roof space was made inhabitable, would make a two bedroomed gite. The forge and small single room unit would be combined to make another two bedroomed gite and, finally, the pig sty would make a third gite. The whole project with interruptions through lack of finance, took eight years!!

My learning curve took another turn when Bob invited me to help with an extraordinary project on a quite small house by the beach near to Lannion. The house was not particularly old and had been built, as a single story house, using an unusual type of block which I had never seen before. The blocks were made of a type of clay and were essentially hollow. The result was a block, similar in size to a breeze block, which made a perfectly functional wall in terms of supporting the roof but was very fragile if hit, for example, with a hammer. This meant that it was very difficult to attach anything to the wall using conventional screw and plug fittings. The owner had determined that, since the sloping roof was high enough to accommodate a second floor, it should be possible to make two bedrooms in the roof space. It was obvious; however, that the clay brick walls would not support a timber floor for the bedrooms and Bob decided that the only way it could be done was to support the new floor on free standing vertical wooden beams rather like building a box within a box.
This constituted some of the finest engineering in timber that I had ever seen since any dimensional errors would leave the bedroom floors unsupported! The whole project took several weeks but, when it was finished, the end result was a beautiful

gite only fifty metres from the beach.

By the beginning of my third summer my gite cleaning business was growing nicely and, with the help of my earlier contacts, I was developing a reputation which meant that gite owners were finding me by recommendations from existing clients. Some of the work was very basic since the gites were already established although most of them were in unusual locations like one which was next door to a farm which bred alpacas and mother and I always enjoyed watching them and chatting to the owner of the farm. We had one memorable occasion when we arrived to prepare the gite just in time to see a tiny newborn alpaca struggling to stand up for the first time and we watched it taking its first drink from its mother, a very emotional experience. There were several Gites situated in the centre of villages but most were in open countryside having been built, like my own house, as farm worker's homes. The only problem was that my "territory" now covered an area of forty miles, from one end to the other, which was difficult to service if we had three or four change-overs on one day. Added to this, the garden maintenance work, in the summer season, was keeping me fairly busy although it meant I could afford to buy better and more efficient garden machinery such as mowers, strimmers and even a couple of chain saws.

It was on one of my garden maintenance days that I met a man who was to have a profound influence on my life and philosophy. I had been asked, by my client, to remove some concrete garden edging slabs and put them into the van of a visiting friend so that he could use them in his garden. Since the house had no access to the rear garden, I had to carry them through the house so could not avoid meeting Dudley for the first time. He was in his late sixties with white balding hair and an otherwise unspectacular appearance but what would have been described as a "posh" accent, speaking slowly and deliberately. He had arrived at my client's house in his van, a ten year old Japanese van which looked as though it had stopped growing at an early age and had a carrying capacity of around 5 cwt with an appropriately small engine. I assumed that his attraction to my client had distracted him somewhat since he insisted on calling me Peter and spoke to me as though I was a common gardener, which I was, of course, but didn't need reminding. I didn't like being called Peter and, since I wasn't going to get any help loading the concrete, I decided to stack the slabs just inside the back of the van so that, by the time I had finished, the front wheels of the van were hardly touching the road!! Next time we meet, he will probably get my name right.

CHAPTER SIX

Dudley

Only two days later, I was put on my guard when the telephone rang at home.
"Ah, hello Tony, Dudley here"
Oh no, his van must have broken on the way home and now he is after my blood!
"Hello, Dudley, how are you?"
I held my breath wondering what I would hear next.
"Margaret tells me that you are a handy chap to have around and I wondered if you could come over, some time, and help me with a few jobs" !!
Phew.
Obviously, I was very relieved and pleased to receive directions from him on how to find his house which was thirty miles or so inland. He suggested that, since it was a bit of a trek to get there, we should come for the day and devise a plan of attack so we arranged a suitable date and Mother and I set off, armed with tools and sandwiches.
Fortunately, Dudley's directions took us easily to his house and we arrived mid-morning. His house was, like most country houses, an old farm worker's house just fifty metres from the main farm house and with its own acre of land attached.
There was an old barn made from substantial timbers and covered in corrugated metal sheeting with an open front. This was useful for storing firewood and tools plus Dudley's ride-on mower and his small van which seemed to have survived its journey laden with concrete slabs. We were invited into his house and given the guided tour.
The house had extensions built onto the back and one end which remained in an unfinished condition since Dudley bought the house. There was also a very tight staircase leading upstairs to two bedrooms whilst the ground floor, of the original part of the house, had one room which Dudley used as his study containing several hundred books and a music centre with even more C.D.s .
The main room had a large open fire, obviously original Breton, an old dining table and a stone sink with kitchen units and cooker besides. The condition of the interior of the house confirmed that Dudley lived alone in true "bachelor" fashion with every corner of every room stacked with what most people would describe as rubbish and yet it all looked as though it was frequently used. Most of his pots, pans and crockery seemed to be scattered around the kitchen worktops. One could easily imagine that the farmer's mice had no trouble finding shelter in the winter!

When we arrived, Dudley had been potting out small vegetable plants and filling seed trays with compost so his dining table looked more like a garden centre counter. Nevertheless, we were offered tea and coffee and the plants were pushed to one end of the table so that there was space for cake and biscuits!

We chatted, over coffee, and Dudley outlined his plans for his house. He was most concerned about his garden and orchard and, since he had no D.I.Y. skills, needed help in building a greenhouse in his barn and then he wanted to convert the "extension" on the back of his house into a ground floor bedroom that he could use for himself instead of having to struggle to get up his dangerous staircase. Most of these old farm worker's houses were designed to use the ground floor as living space and the roof space for crop and food storage so, when staircases were installed, they were invariably steep and in confined spaces which meant that, as you got to the top of the stairs, you were immediately confronted by the roof timbers. This was never a problem for most true-born Breton people since they were normally quite short in stature, like me, but very strong and stocky in build, unlike me. Dudley, on the other hand, was tall enough to bang his head before reaching the top step, hence the desire for a ground floor bedroom with his own bathroom.

In view of the project and the travelling distance between my house and his, we agreed that it was best if Mother and I came over for one full day per week until the work was completed.

Over the following months, we became very friendly with Dudley and I was especially please that, since he was only a couple of years younger than Mother, they seemed to "bond" to the extent that I might hope that Mother had found her much needed soul mate. Naturally, there were aspects of Dudley's personality which left a little to be desired, not least of which his sense of hygiene. Mother never quite accepted the idea of Dudley cutting the green mould off of his cheese before putting it onto his bread which had small amounts of potting compost mixed in with the butter. Nevertheless, as the weeks went by, we got to know Dudley as a friend and always enjoyed his tales about his working life when he had been an antiques dealer and, ultimately, a chicken sexer!! Apparently, when chickens hatch, their sex is not immediately obvious except to an expert and most farmers had to pay for an expert to sort out the men from the girls since only the latter would supply eggs whilst the former were needed to protect the continuation of the species. An unusual profession for an unusual man, one might say.

In his "barn" outside he had two enormous chest freezers where he stored his frozen meat. Apparently, once or twice per year, he would go back to England in his little van to visit his sons and to stock up with "proper" English meat, he didn't trust the "French Muck"!

Most people, in our area, knew Dudley and liked him and this list included our Clairvoyant friend, our estate agent friend and our friend with the wealthy Parisian builder friend. Dudley had a natural "air" about him which most women, including Mother, found attractive. Living alone, as he did, he enjoyed drinking wine and whiskey and, although he didn't smoke to excess, he enjoyed "the odd cigarette". During the second winter of our friendship, Dudley became unwell with a rather nasty, chesty cough so, whilst on one of his return visits to England, he went to see a doctor and was sent for x-rays. The results were, perhaps, a little vague but they reported a shadow on one of his lungs. Dudley was, naturally, very worried and most subdued on his return to France. So, after a couple of weeks, he went to a local G.P. and explained the problem. The French system is quite different to the English N.H.S in that one does not have to register with a G.P., instead, you can go to any doctor for treatment but you have to pay at the time of the interview and, subsequently, for any treatment or medication. You then have to claim against your insurance, if you have any, or on a system which existed at that time known as E111. On the positive side, treatment is immediate so in a couple of days, Dudley had an in-depth report on the French x-rays and he was in much brighter form when he arrived home that afternoon.

"It's only Bloody Pneumonia" He told us and, naturally, we were very relieved for him, Mother was so pleased she kissed him!! I couldn't remember seeing Mother kiss a man since my Father's death.

Work was suspended for the rest of the day and we all went into the kitchen, cleared the plant pots and compost to one side and Dudley opened a bottle of wine for me and a bottle of whiskey for himself in celebration whilst Mother made herself a cup of tea. We chatted for an hour, or so, and agreed to come back, to resume work, next week. We shook hands and mother gave him another kiss and we drove off home.
That was the last time we saw Dudley

We did our day's work, the next day, and were just about to prepare dinner when the telephone rang. It was our friend Anna and she was obviously crying. She had been to Dudley's house that morning and found him dead at the bottom of his stairs, with a broken neck. We were, needless to say, shocked and horrified and Mother burst into tears but there was nothing we could say or do.
Poor, poor Dudley had, apparently, finished celebrating with his bottle of whiskey and, instead of going to bed in his newly completed ground floor bedroom, had, we guessed, gone upstairs to bed and fallen backwards down the stairs. We could only hope that the end was instant and that he felt no pain. Mother and I hardly spoke that evening.

Needless to say, Dudley's two sons came over to France the next day and called Anna, Mother and me to go to Dudley's house to discuss the situation. None of us wanted to meet under such circumstances but arrangements had to be made for his funeral and the house had to be cleared and secured. Most people have to deal with the effects of losing a loved one, we had dealt with the loss of my Father some fifteen years earlier, but the task is always very hurtful and almost eerie when one has to deal with even the most basic tasks like throwing away food and old newspapers or emptying the refrigerator and his two enormous freezers which he had only recently filled.

Anna took charge of the funeral arrangements and it was decided that, since Dudley so loved his life in France, he should be buried in the nearby village of Logivy Plougras but the funeral had to be delayed by a few days to allow time for Dudley's many friends to assemble.

I had been asked, by Dudley's sons, to be one of the coffin bearers at his funeral so Mother and I arrived at the Church in good time and waited for the hearse to arrive. By the time of the funeral, most of Dudley's friends had arrived and we had all expressed our condolences.

Imagine our surprise when a builder's van pulled up outside the Church and took the only parking space in front of the main doors! Apparently, the builder, being another of Dudley's friends had insisted on making his contribution so he had taken his tools out of the van and given it a quick clean....... Dudley was inside his coffin, inside the van!

Despite everything, we all smiled and reflected on how Dudley would have enjoyed travelling in such style. The four coffin bearers, including myself, gathered at the back of the van and struggled to get the coffin out, Dudley was not a small person so the whole was very heavy and our task was not made any easier by the fact that the other bearers were a local farmer and his two sons. The farmer was, like me, a short man of some fifty years or so whilst his two sons were best described as "strapping blokes". Nevertheless, we got Dudley out of the van and up to shoulder height, the farmer and I on the front and the sons at the rear so that the coffin proceeded into the Church at a somewhat unsteady angle of around fifteen degrees from the horizontal.

This meant, of course, that the farmer and I really did get the heaviest end so, by the time we got to the Altar, both farmer and I were struggling and were looking rather red in the face,

The service was a fitting tribute to our friend, many kind things being said and the loss we all felt being well expressed. Then the struggle to get him back into the van for the short drive to the Cemetery which was on a hilltop just outside the village. Everything had been prepared for Dudley's burial and the coffin was put in position with two sturdy ropes placed underneath. The last words were said and the four of us took up the ropes, the boards were removed and the four of us gently lowered my old friend into his final resting place. There is no more final a goodbye than this and we all cried unashamedly.

Mother and I took the next day off to recover and Dudley's two sons visited us briefly before going back to England.

During the following two weeks, Mother and I noticed what might be described as an atmosphere in my house with occasional "noises" in the evening, rather like someone moving around upstairs and, every now and then, banging on the bedroom floor directly above our lounge. I checked on the first couple of occasions but saw nothing.

Then we started to get the feeling that we were not alone when travelling in the car to and from work. Ultimately, my driver's side car door flew open whilst we were driving along the motorway…

Our situation took another turn when we arrived home at the end of that day and, within minutes, received a telephone call from one of my clients who worked as a clairvoyant, she also knew Dudley.

"Have you heard from Dudley?" She asked with a tone of concern in her voice..

"Dudley is dead." Was my brief reply.

"Have you heard from Dudley?" She asked again, more forcefully this time.

"I don't know what we have heard or who it is from but there is certainly something strange going on. Why?"

She explained that, in her experience as a clairvoyant, she sometimes received "messages" from the recently deceased and Dudley had told her that he had had a disagreement with a lady, particularly dear to him, in recent weeks and he needed me to help resolve the situation. I asked why he should have chosen me and was told that he trusted me to deal with the matter sensitively. My head started to spin, I am just an ordinary chap with no experience in such matters and, whilst I firmly believe in God, I have certainly never even considered the idea of communication after death.

Since I knew the Lady in question, as well as the basic details of the misunderstanding, I agreed to help, if only to give Dudley the peace he deserved.

I went, the next day, to see the Lady concerned and explained, as delicately as I could, the situation which was preventing his peaceful departure. Thankfully, my explanation was accepted, all be it with a little surprise about my "inside knowledge" of the affair and the Lady concerned was satisfied and relieved to think that Dudley was, indeed, the honourable man she had always thought him to be.

Had it not been for the fact that I was personally involved in these events, I would never have believed such a story but it is true and I remember well my feelings of satisfaction and pride in being able to contribute to Dudley's final peace. God bless you, Dudley, and goodbye.

CHAPTER SEVEN

More Learning Curve

By the spring of the next year, my horse, Emmy was three years old and ready to move onto a more fulfilled life. I was, now, able to ride her for short distances and borrowed a spare saddle from Dominique but she had no shoes so we were restricted to using the bridle path opposite my house. She was, I found, very intelligent and was the only horse I have ever known which I could mount, bare back, (the horse, not me) and, with only a head collar and lead rope, would walk and trot around the field and even, if asked, walk backwards.

I contacted Dominique to ask him if he could find a buyer so he suggested that we take her to his field for convenience. Emmy and I had developed a strong bond and even enjoyed a form of embrace which involved my hugging her neck whilst she wrapped her front leg around my legs. When we took her to Dominique's house and I said goodbye to her, Dominique's wife's eyes filled with tears as she watched our final embrace, something else they had not seen in a man /horse relationship. Within two weeks, Emmy had been sold and went to live with a handicapped boy and his family and, once she had bonded with the boy, she would let him curl up next to her in her stable and they would snooze together.

The release of more capital meant that I could afford a bigger car and I was lucky enough to meet a retired English couple who were going back to England and wanted to sell their Renault 19 diesel estate car. This was ideal since I now had quite a collection of garden tools and had inherited Dudley's ride on mower so, with a trailer I had bought from another English friend, I could take the mower with me and cut larger lawns more quickly, a very necessary facility as my garden workload increased with each new client.

As summer approached, I was offered a job replacing the slate roof tiles on a holiday home in nearby St Clet. This was something of an undertaking but I knew that Vikki was coming to stay with us again and she could help mother so easing the burden for us all. Getting the old slates off was not too difficult since I still had my access tower and the slates could be lowered, by the bucket full, so that mother could empty them into the trailer. Unfortunately, the timber boards that supported the slates were "dodgy" to say the least so it was necessary to fit lines of thin wooden strips onto the boards to provide me with an even base for the new slates. Once the new slates were delivered, the real work started and mother and I were more than grateful for Vikk's arrival. We soon had a system operating where mother filled the bucket with slates and Vikki carried them up the scaffold where I took them to the roof and secured them with French hooks.

The whole operation had passers by stopping to watch the spectacle of a 74 year old woman passing slates to a 16 year old girl who was carrying them up the scaffold to me, three generations working as one! Things went well until, for the final couple of metres up to the top of the roof, then the weather decided, as it should in late July, to get hot, very hot. The slates became almost too hot to handle so we had to wear gloves, then to add to the fun, the owner arrived and took charge. The first move was to send mother and Vikki home, then, as we got to the point of fitting the ridge tiles, he decided we should secure them with his own idea of " strong " cement. The problem was that, by the time he had mixed his special formula and carried it to the top of the roof, it was beginning to set in the bucket! The end result was that our carefully fitted slates were topped off with an unsatisfactory capping which would have been likely to let in the rain and, needless to say, it rained very heavily in September so I had my first and only dissatisfied client although the villagers of St Clet had enjoyed four weeks of free entertainment.

As autumn approached and the gite season slowed down, we were able to look forward to a little more social time since I now had ten gites to look after and things had been pretty hectic during the summer. We had been invited to a social evening at the home of a friend of a friend. There we met a very charming lady whose husband had been a senior officer in the RAF and they had bought their house intending to retire to France once his career ended with the Air Force. Unfortunately, when the time came, he decided not to live in France whilst his wife, a qualified teacher, had already found work in nearby Lannion and was happy to stay in Brittany, she had decided to convert the "barn" into an apartment so that her parents could come to France to live where she could look after them. There was also a workers cottage on the property which had been previously made into a gite and provided extra income. The barn was an unusual building in two halves, one with walls, the other open and the whole joined by a first storey, and quite large, roof space. I was invited to help with the conversion. The first job was to make the roof space inhabitable starting by fitting velux roof windows and internal walls to make a bedroom and bathroom. Whilst this was being done a local English builder, not called Bob, was creating walls around the open part of the ground floor so that a kitchen and lounge could be created. I was then asked to put tiles on the floor and around the kitchen and bathroom. More learning curve.

I was also pleased to meet her three children the youngest, a boy, was very pleasant and polite and enjoyed helping out when he was not at school. The middle child, a girl, had very quickly adapted to French life and was already enjoying the French boys who were instantly taken by her natural beauty and personality. The oldest girl, Lydia, had an extraordinary air about her and I found myself almost struck dumb from the first time she glided into the room. She was, I guess, around sixteen years old when we first met and had come to live with her mother, in France, where she could complete her education in the French system which is, apparently, better than the English GCSE. Not only did she learn the language and adapt to the education system, she got first class results in every exam she took and so was able to choose which university she would go to finish her education. She is, obviously, very intelligent as well as beautiful. Viv also introduced us to another of her many friends who had their holiday home in a nearby village and had been impressed by my work on Viv's barn so I was asked to do some floor tiling in their house as well as taking charge of their garden. The flooring was completed so I was asked to create a bathroom in an outbuilding attached to the house. This was going to be my first plumbing work, I had watched the French plumbers and had helped my friend Bob but, somehow, working alone was something quite different. The work, nevertheless, went fairly smoothly and within the French regulations so the client was quite satisfied and pleased to recommend me to his friends.

After a quiet December, we were looking forward to Christmas and were especially delighted when Vikki called to say she was coming over between Christmas and new year to be with us during her school break. All we needed to do was meet her at the ferry port at St Malo on the day after boxing day. We were, by now, getting used to the drive to St Malo so we set off at the usual time but were not too happy about the weather. The locals had told us that it only snowed in Brittany once every seven years or so, needless to say, it was about time and the drive home was a little more stressful than usual as the first flakes of snow started to fall. We were not surprised, therefore, to wake up the next morning with four or five inches of snow covering everything and, because it was windy, some ominous looking snow drifts so, for the first time since she left, I was pleased not to have to worry about my horse. Fortunately, since Vikki was with us, we could take a few days off work and relax, driving in the snow was not a serious problem to me having driven fairly frequently in the English winters but the poor French drivers had more serious problems with many young drivers having to drive for the first time in these conditions. As we drove the four miles to visit our friends Jack and Mary, we passed three cars already buried in the road side ditches so Mary's daughter Anne Marie was especially pleased to be reunited with Vikki since Jack was "not good at driving in the snow".

We enjoyed our week with Vikki but it wasn't until the day before she was due to go home that the snow cleared sufficiently for the tractors to recover the ditched lorry and several cars so that our road was once again open to traffic and we were able to drive back to St Malo.

The tourists started to arrive early, that year, and I found myself plunged into an intensive language improvement regime. One of the first groups to arrive wanted to go horse riding so I asked my friend Dominique where we could go and he recommended a riding centre on the other side of the valley from my own home and gave me directions on how to find it. It was situated on the edge of the Foret De Lancerf which is the largest commune owned forest in Brittany and, as such, open to public access. I went there to have a look around before taking my tourists and was introduced to the owners Jack and Edith who showed me around the site. There was a row of stables which ran alongside a large hangar sized building with more stables inside and a central area where various farm machines were parked, on the other side were the various tack rooms. Along the far end of this building was a row of rooms on the ground floor and more rooms on the first floor where the owners lived. There were also two or three extra bedrooms where the yard staff, mostly girls, lived during the short summer holiday season between the beginning of July and mid September. The ground floor rooms included an office area and a well fitted kitchen which served both for owners, staff and clients. Outside, at the "residential" end was a fenced ménage area with earth and woodchip floor surface where lessons were held for the youngest children and other novices. The remainder of the main building was surrounded by fenced grazing areas. By the side of this area, and only one hundred yards or so from the residence, was a medium sized oval track which, I was told was used for training and exercising a number of race horses which were either owned by Jack and Edith or stabled there for other owners. They were also pleased to tell me that, once per year, they held a full two day race meet which, they said, was not to be missed. Since the whole site was situated on the edge of the forest, they were able to access the many bridle paths and take organised riding groups for one or two hour hacks every day throughout the season.

Whilst Edith gave the appearance of being a very attractive city lady, her husband Jackie was, obviously, an ex-jockey in both height and his approach to horses. Edith, I later learned, was a Paris based accountant whose involvement with horses had caused her to meet Jackie and both she and her daughter had horses at Coat Bruc where her daughter spent her holiday seasons taking out groups of riders into the forest. The forest itself covered several square miles running alongside the river Trieux estuary almost as far as Lezardrieux so providing some really spectacular views as well as some exciting gallops as one returned inland back towards Coat Bruc.

This was clearly "the place to go" when I was asked to take my tourists horse riding. It was also another help with my ever growing language skills as I learned to translate for my tourists who were all invited to put on and take off the horses tack, saddle, etc, as well as grooming both before and after the ride. This was a truly great way to learn to speak French.

As my friendship with Jackie developed, I was able to spend more time there, after hacking out with my tourists, but was a little concerned on one occasion when, as I arrived, Jackie asked me if I would help out with a "little operation" they were about to carry out on one of their race horses in readiness for their annual race meeting. struggled to understand as he explained that his horse, a mare, was suffering with air being drawn into its womb when at full gallop and the only prevention was to temporarily stitch up the horse's vagina!! The horse was given a local anaesthetic so that it remained conscious throughout and two of us had to stand by the horse's head holding its head collar and a snaffle to make sure that it didn't move whilst Jackie applied the stitches! Thankfully, the operation went smoothly and the horse suffered no problems. I, on the other hand, went home a much older and wiser man with even greater language skills!!

When the day of the race meet arrived, mother and I were invited to go along as guests and were more than impressed to see the number of spectators as well as the wide range of attractions including a fantastic display of very ancient diesel and steam powered working farm machinery. Since neither mother nor I had been to a horse race meeting before, we weren't quite sure what to expect so we were a little surprised to discover, as we approached the track, that the secure fencing was on the inside of the track and the spectators were only protected from the horses by a length of rope around the outside! We had a programme and were eagerly awaiting the first race which was for novices, including youngsters who looked to be only just in control of their mounts as they thundered by us only ten feet or so away and were so close that we felt the ground, beneath our feet, tremble. This was exciting but the second race was another matter, it was a trotting race with the horses pulling flimsy looking two wheeler carriages with the driver sitting on the carriage with his legs spread apart overlapping the horses rear legs and the horse rushing at great speed in an extended trot. We had seen this sport on the television but, standing so close to the track, could never have imagined how exciting it is to watch and feel the eight or ten trotting teams coming hurtling by at such speed.

The whole event passed smoothly except for one rather tense moment when one of the trotters overturned his carriage half way round the bend nearest to the spectators. Fortunately no one was hurt and the jockey was declared fully recovered after a couple of cigarettes and a glass of red anaesthetic (vin de pays, I think). There were several judged events going on in the middle of the track but we decided not to risk crossing the track to see them and ended our superb afternoon of entertainment with an ice cream before setting off on the four mile drive home.

In a later conversation, with my friend Anna, when we were relating the story of the race meeting, she told us about another annual event we might like to visit. Apparently, once per year, there is a horse race meeting on the beach near to Plestin Les Greves and it was well worth a visit. Obviously, since the meeting had to be run at low tide, it only lasted two or three hours so we arrived in good rime and secured a view point "on dry land". The locals are not, normally, very good at slick organisations or prompt starts but this one had to be an exception and, sure enough, the track was roped off and the first race started on time. The track was a fairly short and simple oval with the start and finish straight nearest to the main road which ran alongside the beach at this point so, once again, we enjoyed the thrill of being close to the horses as they raced by us and could hear both horses and riders breathing at enormous rates even above the cheers of the spectators.

According to the programme, two of the mid session races were hurdle races and we wondered how on earth they were going to put hurdles up on the sandy beach. Imagine, then, our surprise to see three portable hurdles, two on the back straight and one by the start line, being wheeled into place for the start of the races. Not only were they set right across the width of the track, but the hurdle on the start/finish straight was positioned directly on the finish line! The flag dropped to start the first race and the horses immediately jumped the first hurdle, as they rounded the first bend, they began to line up for the two hurdles on the back straight and rounded the second bend to head for the third hurdle. Over they went and we began to wonder if the finish of the race was going to be airborne since the hurdle was on the finishing line. Not a bit of it, as soon as they had all cleared the hurdle to start the last lap, a group of young locals rushed on to the track and pushed the hurdle out of the way so revealing the finishing line. Only the French would think of something so simple!

It was around this time that our friend Lolita decided that she would expand her horizons and convert one of her outbuildings into a temporary residence for herself so that she could rent out her main house to groups and large families as well as letting her gite during the summer season. So Bob and I set about creating a living area within what had once been an animal store and, more recently, a junk store.

It took a month or so despite the fact that she had elected to keep the feed troughs. Fortunately she had spent much of her working life in England living in a farming environment so she actually enjoyed "slumming it" especially with the enhanced privacy she found once installed. One of the early "group lettings" was to an English classical music orchestra and I was asked to take them to Coat Bruc for an afternoon of riding in the forest which we all enjoyed although some of the less experienced riders had trouble walking the next day!

Having once been a busy port and industrial area, Pontrieux had two railway stations, one in the centre of the town, purely for passengers, and the other by the side of the port. The railway line itself provided a link between Paimpol, on the coast, and the town, further inland, with the unpronounceable name of Guingamp (Gangomp). The section of line between Pontrieux and Paimpol included a two or three mile stretch alongside the river estuary and enjoyed the most breathtaking views of the forest and the Chateau De La Roche Jagu as well as the bridge over the river Trieux at Lezardrieux. A group of rail enthusiasts decided that it would be a great tourist attraction if they could run a steam train between Pontrieux and Paimpol, both stations having ample sidings so that the train could run without disturbing the diesel powered commuter train which ran several times per day. Needless to say, as soon as we heard about the pending three day trial run over Easter, we booked tickets and were thrilled to be carried back in time on the half hour journey to Paimpol as we steamed, smoked and rattled our way along the banks of the Trieux. The locals were equally excited by the idea and spectators had gathered by every road crossing and view point to wave us by, mother was waving back with child like enthusiasm and telling me about her last train journey to the seaside which, we worked out, had been some sixty years earlier!

Once we arrived in Paimpol, we had a half hour break whilst the engineers refuelled the train and checked it over and the enthusiasts, myself included, rushed around taking pictures. On the return trip, we stopped at a "passing point" on the line near to a very large house on the edge of the forest where, we were told, a notorious French murderer had once lived whilst hiding from the police. Back in Pontrieux, the old goods yard was lined with stalls selling souvenirs, sweets and the obligatory wine and beer. The three day trial was so successful that it was decided to run the steam train for the summer season, an event which soon became a "tradition".

By the end of the summer, our friend Lolita had decided that the revenue from her manor house plus the attached gite was not worth the discomfort of living in her converted barn, added to the fact that she was neither as young nor as fit as she used to be. She decided to sell the manor house and bought a row of three very small, one room farm worker's cottages on the other side of St Clet and, with Bob the builder's help, set about making the three small units into one. It took a couple of months of hard work from Bob and me to get the house into an inhabitable condition and Lolita worked hard to try to establish a garden on the acre or so of land surrounding the house. The design for the house was a good one giving her a large kitchen with bedroom and bathroom over whilst the second unit was made into a spacious living room, with wood burning stove, leading to a guest unit with separate kitchen and bathroom plus bedroom created on a mezzanine floor in the roof space. Whilst it was likely to take a year or more to complete the project and to get a garden established, the house soon began to be a home and Lolita quickly settled in with the help of a few of her customary parties and barbeques. Once the building and structural work was complete, she asked mother and me to help organise the land so that she would have a decorative area next to the house, a vegetable garden beyond and surrounding lawns. The land across the road would be a car park.

My clients, up to this point, had all been English but, as my reputation spread, I was introduced to some "foreigners". The first being a French neighbour of a client in the village of Pommerit Jaudy , he had a very large holiday home which, since he was retired, he would visit for the summer season having spent the earlier Easter break getting the house "de -cobwebbed" and the garden tidied up after the winter. This is where I came in. The first time I met him was for the Easter clean up and he took me around his sizeable garden describing the work he wanted me to do and starting off by

cutting back the previous years growth, with an electric hedge trimmer! I suggested that this was rather a harsh way to treat his plants.
"Don't worry" he said with confidence "they will soon grow back."
If we were to treat our gardens like that in England in such a brutal way, the plants would, no doubt, die but, in Brittany, the weather was milder and the sheltered garden provided much more vigorous growth. I was then asked to call every two weeks to keep the lawns cut and to tackle other little updates amongst his flower beds.

Another non-English client who was invited to contact me was a family of Germans who had their holiday home near to the village of Plouec Du Trieux. They rented their house to German tourists during the summer period, this income covered the running costs, and they spent the remaining school holidays there with their two children.

They had, apparently, owned the house for around twenty years and were, by now, accustomed to the ten-hour drive from Frankfurt. I was asked to look after the garden and operate my established "meet and greet" service with the customary clean through of the gite before the guests arrived. Since this was my first opportunity to work for a German owner, I was a little apprehensive about receiving payment for my work as it was too far to go if I had to collect my money. Fortunately, the guests were asked to pay me themselves so I was only paid for my gardening work and the occasional decoration work by the owners. I found them to be very good to work for although somewhat demanding and both mother and I enjoyed an occasional meal with them when we were treated to stories about life in Germany and Samuel's time as a professional footballer. I had wondered about their German tourists and whether they would be as demanding as the owners but I found them to be interesting and pleasant with only one exception. It was high summer and we were enjoying a particularly warm spell when the particular couple arrived for their week long holiday and I did the usual tour of the house and twenty minutes chat about where to find the best shops, beaches, markets etc and then left them with my telephone number in case they needed me. The very next day, they telephoned me in the morning before I had time for breakfast.
"Vee haff flies." he announced, rather abruptly.
"Yes" I replied. The gite was about half a mile into open countryside and had a field of maize on one side and a field of cows on the other, so where was the surprise?
"Vee haff many flies," he insisted. "you must deal viz zem."
"Very well sir, I will come around before lunch with some swatters and some fly spray I have a key to the gite if you want to go out."
. "You must not use fly spray, vee vill be back by fyfe o'clock." End of conversation.
Flies were a constant problem in the Breton summer and mother and I were used to dealing with them so we waited until they had gone out for the day and went to the house armed with the usual tools, fly spray, sticky papers, swatters and a vacuum cleaner. When we arrived we realised straight away why they had the problem, all of the windows were wide open and there were cakes and biscuits, open, on the kitchen

table! Clearly German flies are not allowed into German homes, not theirs, at least. Mother and I closed all the doors and windows and emptied two cans of fly spray, went outside to cut the grass and went back in two hours later to vacuum up the dead flies, job done. We didn't hear any more from that particular couple. One of the better aspects of looking after the tourists is that, if they are nice people, we can enjoy chatting with them and, on occasions, enjoy a meal with them.
If they are not nice people, they will be leaving at the end of the week, so don't worry.

By the end of that particular season, we were both quite tired and looking forward to settling down to working on our house and doing some more renovation work with my friend Bob the builder.No sooner had we finished with the tourists than I received a call from one of my owners to say that their house near the beach at Plouha had been broken into. I went directly to the house to find, thankfully, only a little damage and some small items missing plus the television so I went to the local Gendarmerie to report it and was questioned as though I was the robber before being asked to register a "plainte" so that they could investigate the break in. I met the Gendarms at the house and they wandered around making notes and muttering to each other before coldly declaring that it was probably some local kids up to mischief!! Not exactly csi Miami, I thought to myself so I repaired the damage and reported back to the owner. Imagine my surprise when, only two weeks later, another owner telephoned to say that her house at St Clet had been broken into! The two houses were twenty miles apart so there could be no link other than coincidence and, this time, the damage was much worse and several valuable ornaments had been taken, also most of the china ornaments that remained had been smashed. Again, I went to the local Gendarmerie, again, I was questioned and asked to fill in a Plainte. History continued to repeat itself and, this time, the Gendarms added to the mess by covering most of the furniture with fine black fingerprint dust. This time, however, they declared it was probably youths from Guingamp looking for ways to raise drug money. Things went from bad to worse three or four weeks later when I went to my car in the morning. I had built a lean to stable, at the back of the house, where my horse had lived but, since I sold her, I had been parking my ride on mower on its trailer with the bonnet of my car next to it so that both were sheltered from the late autumn weather. I was horrified to discover that someone had moved my car backwards and stolen the mower and trailer, more surprising was that they had not touched the contents of the car including a small amount of cash and over five hundred pounds of hand tools!! This time, I went to the local Gendarmerie in Pontrieux to report the theft and was more than annoyed to be told that it was probably a local artisan who was trying to stop me from stealing his work!! Three times, I had reported a crime and, three times, no action was taken and we were given a feeble excuse for the unacceptable behaviour of "the locals" of three different communes.

This was my first but not my last "brush" with the notorious French bureaucracy. None of the crimes committed were pursued and I was left with no mower so I had to resort to cutting the grass with a push mower for the rest of the winter, thank goodness for the fact that even Breton grass doesn't grow much in winter.

Fortunately for me, building and renovation work was going well and the "closed season" was a good time for my owners to have those little jobs done. My friend Bob also found work for himself and, often, called on me to help him so we managed to keep going. One of Bob's jobs was for a client he had known for several years who lived in Treguier and had bought an old restaurant in the centre of town which they were going to renovate so that they could live on the upper two floors and run their business on the ground floor. The building itself was one of the older buildings in the town and was constructed with massive timber beams supporting the two floors above the restaurant and the central beam, in what was to become the lounge, had sagged over the years so that we had to create a secondary floor to accommodate the sag. This involved adapting the new floor beams to accommodate the nine inch difference between the side and the centre of the room. Another of Bob's brilliant exercises in woodwork engineering.

Another aspect of the quieter winter season was that a number of my owners would come over to France to do their off season refurbishments and, in some cases, to find new caretakers for their houses which was the time I began to appreciate my growing reputation since it was inevitable that there would be one or two owners who would decide to sell their houses so I might lose two clients and gain three or four. One of my new owners that winter was an accountant who kept his house, with its outbuildings and large garden, in very good order and warned me that some of his summer guests, especially the regular ones, could be rather demanding in terms of the cleanliness of the house. One of the outbuildings contained a snooker table, nets and racquets for tennis, a table tennis table and a small caravan which was used every Easter when the owner and his family would meet up, from various parts of England, to enjoy a rare opportunity to be together and relax. The caravan was only small but would play a major role in my own life some years hence. The owner had been right when he suggested that some of his guests could be demanding and I soon learned that, whilst every guest was entitled to expect good value for money, it was often best to try not to let them "get to me". One example was, when a family arrived for their holiday during a wet and windy week. I had a complaint from them that the fish kettle was too small and the pictures on the lounge walls were nothing more than line drawings of Victorian English horse racing.

"We didn't come all this way to struggle in the kitchen and sit looking at English horses." they complained as though the bad weather was my fault! During that winter, I was introduced to another client who had bought a property in nearby Goudelin which is a traditional farming village that is, mysteriously, split into two parts. The main part contains the usual shops, bar, marie and church whilst, on the opposite side of the main road, which was built as a bypass to the village, is a group of houses gathered around a smaller but much older church. My client had bought a house described as a Longere, most standard farm workers houses were built on a ten meters by five metres base whereas the Longere is fifteen meters long which allows for two separate rooms and a central hall on the ground floor. The house had been part renovated before the owner ran out of money so my client came in with his plan to complete the renovation including a design for the first floor with three bedrooms and bathroom. Since my client worked as a contracts manager on building sites in England, he had very definite ideas on how the work should be done and had already met an English builder living in Brittany so, by the time I arrived on the scene, work had already started on the construction of the internal walls and the English builder had brought his ex business partner over from England to help with the work.

The builder, Steve, was, like most Anglo Philes, a somewhat unusual fellow and some of his ideas and techniques were quite different to those of my friend Bob the builder so it was obviously in my own interests to look, listen and learn.

My client also had plans for the half acre field attached to the house and a local contractor was asked to spend some time, with his digger, levelling the ground immediately next to the house to create a lawn and then clearing the rest of the land to make a "wild" area for his children to let off steam without the risk of damaging anything. By cheerful coincidence, I had another client who wanted to buy some top soil to enable him to reclaim part of his land so "a deal" was done and two clients enjoyed significant improvements to their land at better than a bargain price and the contractor, Jean –Pierre, was delighted to have one days work turned into three, all paid for in cash.

Since I was the only English man who could speak French, my client asked me to find a contractor who could deal with the electrical and plumbing installations. It had been pointed out to us that such work had to be done by a French certificated contractor if the property insurance conditions were to be met and we could not find a French registered English contractor so I asked in my village and was introduced to one of the locals who could start the work needed almost straight away. I had asked two other contractors but neither of them could start the work within at least six months.

It could be reasoned that, if they were fully booked, they must be very popular, conversely, if the third contractor was free to start straight away, he might not be very popular only time would tell. Fortunately for my client, the French operate a system whereby they visit the sight, do all the measurements and then submit a document called DEVIS which is, effectively, a pro – forma invoice and the price shown on the devis cannot be changed unless the client changes the specification. My client accepted the devis and the contractor arrived to begin the "first fix", in other words, the wires and pipes were installed within the walls before final plasterboard sheets were fitted, and then came back to finish the installation after the walls had been plastered. On the several occasions that I asked him why he was doing a particular job

in a particular way, he always pointed to his rules and regulations book in such a way that suggested he could not dare to deviate. I was reminded of an old English saying that suggested that rules were made for the guidance of wise men and the obedience of fools, perhaps it was one of those "cultural differences".
Eventually, the main works were completed and the house was ready to receive its furniture.

My client preferred to buy most of his furniture in England, because of his building contracts there, and so started by bringing his kitchen units along with a friend who was going to help him to fit them. The only trouble was that, being an old stone built house with walls over half a meter thick, none of the walls were either straight or square so the factory made units and worktops all had to be cut and shaped to make them fit into the kitchen. The next job was to tile the floors and again it had to be done to a specific design so the client came over from England with several boxes of super quality beige coloured quarry tiles and asked if I could fit them. The problem was that they were only six inch square and he wanted them to be laid in a staggered pattern so that the odd shaped walls did not affect the pattern on the tiles, oh, and there were two and a half thousand of them!

It seemed, at times, as though mother and I would never finish the job since every row needed edge tiles to be cut and shaped around the base of the staircase, door frames and kitchen units, the whole area then had to be grouted, cleaned, and finished. Thankfully, when finished, the effect was very good and my client was so pleased with the result that he decided to finish the effect with cast iron wood burning stoves in both rooms which were to stand on green slate hearths. Even today, I find it hard to believe that, with Mother's help, I could ever have done such work.

During the same winter, I was introduced to another client who had bought a very small house in the centre of Gouldelin village. It was, like most of these old houses, the style of house which suggested that someone had decided to build it onto the end of a row of four town houses. Probably around 200 years ago, so it had one room on each of three floors and no land at all, not even a rear garden. In fact, there were no windows on the rear or the end wall and only one door on the front which opened directly onto the street. The owner worked as an aircraft design engineer so his design for the renovation was laid out with military precision and would result in a very pleasant living room with kitchen and one large bedroom with bathroom upstairs whilst the attic would be locked off from the main rooms and used as a store room. The most difficult part, for me, in creating the rooms was in engineering a turn in the staircase to the first floor, this was really a job for my friend Bob but he was back in England by this time so I consulted with an English man I had met on an earlier renovation. This man had bought an old manor house near to the village of Brelidy and had converted some of the old out buildings into one and two bedroomed apartments so that he had a mixture of bed and breakfast rooms within the manor house plus more private apartments in the outbuildings which completed the square yard opposite the front of the house.

Being a methodical Yorkshire man, he had acquired the official education and documents to allow him to do his own plumbing and electrical installations so, once his own project was complete, he was able to undertake other work to supplement his income. It had made sense, therefore, that once Bob had met him, Tom would become "the man" for our plumbing and wiring needs so I asked him to help on the Goudelin project. Once the walls and staircase were complete, the owner bought a set of English kitchen units for me to fit into the kitchen section of the main room. Unfortunately, the room was not square, in fact it was almost diamond shaped, so the worktops had to be cut quite severely to fit the walls but everything worked well, when it was finished, except for the television which did not receive the French channels and the English transmitter was on the channel islands!!

Since the house had no garden, it had been sold with a half acre plot with lock up garage, both situated on a side street opposite the house, so my client decided that he might apply for planning permission to build a house on the plot and asked me to make the necessary enquiries. I asked the local Maire but he said he was not keen. I felt that perhaps a French owner might not have met with such resistance but had a local architect draw up some plans anyway. A permit was eventually issued but, by that time, the cost of building had escalated beyond my client's budget.

CHAPTER EIGHT

Vikki`s Summer

Nevertheless, my two new clients took my total to twelve gites for the summer so we were set to have a busy season, once the tourists started to arrive.

Our busy summer got off to a bright start and so I was very pleased when my daughter Vikki, arrived to help again with the changeovers. Unfortunately, it was not to work out as I had hoped since Vikki had reached the end of her school education and had no idea of what she wanted to do next so we spent the first few days of her summer in deep discussion about the options available to her. Since her greatest interest was in horses, I decided that we should go up to Coat Bruc and ask Jackie whether he could offer her any work at his stable despite the fact that he had already set on his summer staff and had no spare rooms for Vikki to live on site. After much negotiation and considering the early start to their working day, they agreed to let me put my caravan on site so that Vikki could "give it a go" and see if she would be good enough to satisfy their needs. We were helped by the fact that Vikki already had some ability with the French language so Jackie had the idea that she would be able, at least, to look after the English tourists. On the positive side, the job would last for the six weeks of the holiday season, on the negative side, she would not be paid any money although her food and drink would be provided.

This was not going to be an easy time for Vikki, she would, effectively, be living alone whilst working up to sixteen hours per day and needing mother and I to provide her pocket money, not that she would have time to spend it! Fortunately, the aspect of her personality that made Vikki "her mother's daughter" ruled that she would commit fully to the task and so, within a matter of days, she had settled into the work and had bonded with her new work mates. Although, as I was later told by Edith, during those early times she would often close herself into her caravan at night and cry herself to sleep. Mother and I visited every couple of days and it was good to see how well she was adjusting to horse keeping in the French style. Within a couple of weeks Vikki was taking groups of riders, both English and French, on rides into the forest and helping with lessons for the novices, the children especially enjoyed Vikki's English accent.

Our short summer season flew by and Vikki's time at Coat Bruc seemed to end before it had properly begun so we were a little sad when she told us that there were only two weeks to go despite the fact that she was really quite tired after the long hours of work. The owner's lady, Edith, and her daughter had persuaded Jackie that Vikki deserved a reward for her efforts so she was offered three things as a thank you. The first was an envelope with a modest but very welcome amount of cash, the second an invitation to ride one of the race horses around their track, at full gallop and the third was free use of any two horses for an afternoon ride.

"Come on dad," she said calmly but with a hint of excitement in her voice, "we are going for a ride."

"Are we indeed?" I wondered what I was in for, Vikki knew my riding skills were somewhat limited, I hadn't started horse riding until I was forty years old, so the idea of riding out with my very capable but some what adventurous daughter was just a little daunting.

I arrived at two in the afternoon and Vikki was ready to go with both horses saddled up, her chosen horse was a very strong looking race horse and I was to ride her favourite hacking horse which was around two hands taller than anything I was used to.

"Where are we going?" I asked nervously " I don't fancy the idea of getting lost in the forest on a strange horse."

"You're going to have to trust me, dad, we're going to have fun."

So off we went into the forest which, of course, Vikki now knew well and, within ten minutes, our bridle path had reached the edge of the forest which ran along side the Trieux Estuary. The views were breathtaking as we looked down on to the railway line which mother and I had taken on the steam train the previous summer and, on the opposite bank, the farmhouses and then the Chateau De La Roche Jagu seemed so beautiful in the bright August afternoon sunlight.

Later, we were approaching the northern end of the forest and, rounding a bend, caught site of the bridge at Lezardrieux which we had previously seen from the river when we were in Guy's boat. It was all so stunningly beautiful that I was reminded of my first visit to Brittany and my eleven o'clock stroll on the beach, I mentioned it to Vikki.

"Stop dreaming, dad, we'd better start to make our way back so lets have a bit of a gallop to wake the horses up."

At that, she turned onto a wide bridle path which lead away from the river, kicked her horse, sat forwards into gallop mode and disappeared!! My horse and I turned instantly and set off in hot pursuit, fortunately, for me, the horse knew what to do and all I needed to do was hang on! During my short time riding horses, I had enjoyed long leisurely rides in the countryside, I had enjoyed an attempt at show jumping and I had especially enjoyed the thrill of riding a horse at full gallop but this was an experience I could never have imagined! We ran for what seemed like an eternity but which only lasted for ten minutes or so and yet I emerged from that gallop with an even greater respect for the miracle that is the horse.

"That was good, wasn't it dad?" Vikki wasn't even out of breath.

"Good" I echoed, " it was incredible, I didn't realise horses could go so fast."

"Well it is a retired race horse!" now she tells me.

The ride came to an end all too soon but we were both pretty tired and needed only a couple of glasses of wine to unwind. I wondered whether to offer a glass of wine or two to the horses but Vikki said that wasn't a good idea.

At the end of Vikki's summer she seemed to be in a much more positive frame of mind so Mother and I were both pleased and proud when she called us from England to say that she had been offered a two year scholarship doing equine studies at Leicester's De Monfort University. Well done and good luck, Vikki and thank you Jackie, Edith and all at Coat Bruc.

As our summer came to an end, I had time to look more closely at my own house at Kerraoul which I had managed to improve, since buying it, so that we had three bedrooms upstairs and our kitchen separated from the lounge by an entrance hall with the spiral staircase. In the lounge we had our wood burning stove and television. We were quite comfortable and had, by this time, grown used to the thundering traffic passing by only twenty feet from the front door I had also, with Bob's help, created a workshop within the old ruin at the end of the house. The trouble was that we really needed to be able to put proper velux type windows into the roof and we wanted to put a patio door on the back wall of the house to let in more light and give us direct access to the field. The problem was that this work would cost almost as much as I had paid for the house in the first place, if the job was to be done properly.

I talked it over with Mother and we agreed that the best thing to do was to try to sell the house and find a larger house in a quieter spot with less land since we had decided that the field was not getting used enough since my friend Dominique no longer needed to keep horses there. House prices were beginning to increase in our area and I had met a French estate agent who suggested that the house was now worth twenty thousand pounds which would show me a twelve and a half thousand pound profit, so I put it up for sale.

During that Autumn, our client, whose restaurant we had worked on in Treguier, had decided to close their ladies clothing shop opposite the Treguier cathederal and had moved their furniture into the apartment over the restaurant. I was asked to help with the final clearing of the shop which only involved moving their smaller belongings, mostly in cardboard boxes, and presented no problems until I fell down the twisty wooden staircase. As I checked around, on the final day, to make sure everything was clear, I found a hidden cupboard, by a window, and looked inside. There, to my astonishment, were a number of body parts and a severed head! As my initial panic subsided, I realised that it was a rather dilapidated old mannequin which had been stashed away in the hidden cupboard and looked as though it had been there for some years. It was love at first sight! I dashed over to the client, asked their permission and promptly carried it, still in pieces, out to my car.

My actions inspired some interesting comments from passers by who were not used to seeing people rushing across the market square carrying a pair of legs, so I didn't linger in my departure. Mother wasn't very impressed either but I managed to repair and reassemble my new mannequin and found a space for her to stand in the entrance hall where she could greet visitors and so guarantee some interesting conversations. I decided to name her Marilyn and promised her that I would buy her some clothes and a wig as soon as I could get to a car boot sale.

My estate agent didn't waste any time in bringing potential buyers to see my house so I took the liberty of asking him, Bernard, how the system worked. Evidently properties were sold either by private advertisements, through an estate agent or through a notaire, in any case, all sale and purchase transactions had to be executed by a notaire who would be appointed by the vendor and all expenses must be paid by the purchaser. Since the notaires usually had a good collection of properties on offer, it was a good place to start looking the only problem was that, since they were going to get the business anyway, they made no effort to find buyers. The estate agent (agence immobilier), on the other hand, only earned a commission on properties they sold so were much more aggressive in their techniques and would often have a list of potential purchasers waiting for the right property to come to the market.

CHAPTER NINE

Paradise?

Before the winter was over, Bernard had found us a purchaser, a French lady living in Rouen, who wanted a holiday home near to the coast so Mother and I set about finding a house to buy. We searched around the local notaires and then looked at what the agence immobiliers had to offer. My eye was caught by a property offered by a new immobilier in Pontrieux, it was in nearby Pommerit Le Vicomte so, since I now had several clients there and it was more central to my other work, we went to have a look. The group of houses surrounding it were near to a beautiful but plain chapel called La Chapelle De Notre Dame De Paradis (Paradise)! The house, itself, was an unusual house situated on a very quiet lane that ran along the edge of a small wooded area. It had obviously been renovated and "improved" over a period of several years since only two walls remained of the original house and the end and roadside walls had been rebuilt using an early version of breeze block with, fortunately, more windows plus an entrance porch with half glazed frontage providing an almost "shop window" appearance. The original stone walled end of the house had been extended in two phases, the first being a six foot wide prefabricated unit which provided the house with a modern bathroom. Beyond this extension was another prefabricated unit which provided a lounge of some fifteen feet long and ten feet wide.

At the end of all this was a twenty feet by thirty feet lock-up garage/ workshop which included the water pump and storage tank that provided water to the house from the well which was in the land which described itself as a garden. The whole plot, of over one hundred feet in length, ran parallel to the lane which looked a little odd and impractical but I decided that, if I built a bedroom for mother in the extension, it would give us plenty of space and a very useful degree of privacy. The workshop would be very practical as well, despite the fact that it had only an earth floor, since there was space inside for my car, trailer, ride on mower and all of the other tools and equipment I had acquired.
The owner of the house, a single man, of around seventy years, suffered some serious illness which meant that he had no vocal chords and had to take his nourishment, in liquid form directly into his stomach by tube so he had to live in a care home in the centre on Pommerit Le Vicomte. Consequently, he was pleased to accept my offer of eighteen thousand pounds which left me with enough money to pay the notaires fees. Job done.

Moving house was not particularly difficult since most of our smaller items fitted either into the estate car or onto the trailer and my German "digger" friend Sven, had a van which took the main items of furniture. Both Mother and I were a little sad to leave Kerraoul, its memories and beautiful views behind us but were also looking forward to living in a larger house with central heating.

By the time I had created Mother's new bedroom, my oldest daughter Philippa had announced that she was coming to visit us for only the second time. This was exciting news for us since Philippa and her new man, Duncan had produced Mother's first great grand child and my first grand child, Taylor, and we would now have a chance to get to know her. My friend, Dominique, had agreed to buy Philippa's horse and an acquaintance of mine wanted a horse taken to England so they had hired a horse box and, somewhat courageously, set out to do the exchange but had only three days to do it all before Duncan had to get back to work. Nevertheless, our new house had more space to accommodate our visitors and it was good to see Taylor's progress and to get our family news from England. One of our recent acquaintances in Pommerit was the husband and wife team who owned the hotel, bar and restaurant opposite the church in the village centre so I asked if they could prepare a takeaway "fruits de mer" meal so that we could eat at home and introduce Philippa, Duncan and Taylor to the wonder of our local seafood.

"Leave it to me," said Derek when I phoned him about the meal "we had a wedding lunch earlier today so I can bring the left-overs."

I was not impressed, I couldn't imagine that my family would enjoy rummaging through bowls of abandoned prawns and lettuce.

I could not have been more wrong! It was almost eight o'clock before Derek arrived and ordered us to clear the table, clearly Derek's idea of left overs didn't match mine. The display of seafood would have impressed royalty and neither Philippa nor Duncan had seen such a spread before including a few shellfish they didn't even recognise. It took the five of us two hours to clear the table and even mother enjoyed discovering new flavours and textures, the star feature being "huitre farcie" which is best described as oysters cooked on a bed of rock salt and covered with garlic butter and grated cheese, a truly memorable meal.

It was with a measure of trepidation that we waved goodbye to our visitors, the next day, since they had a long journey ahead of them with a large horse which they didn't know in a trailer they hadn't towed before. Thankfully, they arrived safely and without serious problem.

As our summer approached, we were beginning to settle in to our new home and enjoy the benefits of having more living space whilst, at the same time, discovering some of the less attractive aspects of living on a long thin plot of land sandwiched between the woods to the rear and the lane to the front.

Nevertheless, the central heating, luxury bathroom and spacious workshop left us in no doubt that we had made the right move until, that is, we had a dry spell in the spring and our well water ran dry! It is odd but, since we were used to having town water on tap, when the well ran dry we were lost. I determined, the next day, to have town water connected and set about finding the roadside pipe so that we could have a meter installed. This done I devised a switching system so that I could use the free well water, when it was available, and then switch to town water when the well was dry. Obviously, one never drank either well or town water since bottled drinking water was so cheap, when bought from the supermarket, that it simply was not worth the risk of drinking the nitrogen enriched tap water.

Having an entrance porch on the front of the house meant that we had somewhere to leave our muddy boots and wet coats, it also gave me somewhere to stand my beloved mannequin Marilyn who was, by now, properly dressed and stood waving to passers by. This inspired some interesting comments, once people had realised that she was not a real person that is, and it was fun to watch older walkers and mothers with young children who would often stop to say hello and even wave back to her. Then there was the occasion when the army had organised a military exercise for a troop of around twenty men, in the woods behind our house, although we barely noticed them until they had finished and were in the process of marching past our house, guns akimbo, as they spotted Marilyn in the window, the first two or three were startled and took a grasp of their guns but the remainder saw the humorous side and either saluted or simply waved!

Living in Pommerit was much more interesting, socially, for Mother and me since Derek's bar and restaurant provided a meeting point for both French and English locals so our social circle quickly expanded and, of course, I soon began to get extra work. There were three other bars in Pommerit so a small group of local retired men had a " circuit" of bars which they would visit twice in the morning and two or three times in the afternoon before closing time which was usually around eight o'clock. The village also had a veterinary service, a dentist and several other shops including a super market called 8 a huit, (eight till eight) which opened at half past seven, closed for two hours at lunch time and closed at seven in the evening, obviously one shouldn't believe everything one reads. We also had a builder's merchant and an agricultural supply depot which included a very basic garden centre. We also enjoyed the services of garage Antoine who was one of a rare breed of traditional mechanics who could repair almost anything so it was a very well served village.

By the time we moved into our house at Paradise my German digger friend Sven had been home to Germany for a holiday and returned with his school time girlfriend Hieke who, although very pretty, was extremely thin and frail looking and in complete contrast to Sven who was quite tall and very muscular. The surprise, for me at least, was that, not only did Hieke enjoy horse riding, she had a six hundred Yamaha motor bike which she rode very well once she got it off its centre stand!
During that first summer, one of my new Pommerit clients, an English man, came to

France for his six week summer holiday and bought with him his recently acquired twelve hundred BMW custom touring motorbike and, as soon as he heard about my motor cycling past, gave me the keys and told me it had a tank full of petrol and that I should put it back in the garage when I had finished! This was too good to miss so Hieke and I set off on our motorbikes and spent the afternoon "cruising" around our beautiful coast with only an occasional coffee stop, another of those unforgettable events. I quickly bonded with our local garagiste when one of our tourists had a fault with his car which was a very collectable Triumph sports car which had brake failure. Despite the fact that it was British and almost thirty years old, Antoine found a set of brake pads and fitted them the same day so we were all suitably impressed.

One of the minor disturbances during our busy summer season was that a growing number of first time tourists fell in love with Brittany and asked about the possibility of buying their own property with a view to renting it out during the summer season. The only problem with this idea is that the existing owners would lose their business next year and, since there were soon to be more gites available, there would effectively be fewer lets to go round. Nevertheless, I was able to earn extra money helping them to find properties, which were still quite cheap at that time, and I therefore soon developed some new contacts within the local agence immobiliers and notaires. The other advantage was that, if the tourist did find a property to buy, I would normally be asked to translate for the purchase and, later, organise the renovation although, if I did the translation, I needed to be accurate since an error on my part could cost somebody a lot of money and I had to be sure that, if renovation work was done in my absence, all appropriate certification was in order. This new level of work meant that my command of the French language was becoming better than I had ever imagined although a reduction in spare time and therefore social activities meant that my social diction was not keeping up.

During that first summer in Paradise we had another visit from my old school friend and his wife, they had visited us at Kerraoul and, like most visitors, decided that they too would like to buy a holiday home in Brittany so I mentioned it to my friend Anna she immediately offered him a house near to Guerlesquin which had been abandoned by an English couple who had run out of money. We went to look at the house and my friends were immediately impressed by the position, size, and condition of the house, then we were shown the land. The house itself, was in a small group of houses, as normal, gathered around a large farmhouse but was situated on a small hilltop with a river valley behind so that the "garden" extended all the way down hill to the river with a number of small terraces each lined with an assortment of trees. The house fronted on to a private lane, used only by the farmer, and had, on one side, an old ruin which was part of the sale and, on the other side, a holiday home which belonged to a Frenchman and his family so the area was very pleasant and quiet. The decision to buy was easily made since the house, itself, could be lived in whilst the renovation work was carried out and there would be an ample supply of firewood to keep it heated, all that was needed, of importance, was a sceptic tank which my friend Sven was pleased to install. The renovation work inside was soon under way and my friend and his wife were able to spend time there during the school holidays and would bring furniture and fittings with them whenever they came over.

The main advantage with the house was that someone had built an extension on the back of the house which virtually doubled the ground floor area of the original building so they created a kitchen/diner area in one half of the extension and a guest bedroom with ensuite bathroom in the other half. This left space for two more bedrooms and another bathroom in the roof space so, within one year of buying the house, they had a near perfect holiday home for the price of a new family saloon car!

The summer seemed to pass at an alarming rate, mainly because looking after twelve gites meant that we seemed to be forever working, so it was late Autumn before I was able to organise my own social evening, the first time we had done this sort of thing. As soon as I suggested that we were going to have a house warming party with barbeque, our friends started suggesting things we could do in terms of putting canvas shelters on the lawn and they each arrived, on the night, with tables, chairs, crockery, glasses, cutlery and everything else needed so I just left them to it and enjoyed a superb evening which ended up as a floodlit garden party which was enjoyed by everyone including the new neighbours who had "walked in" carrying their own wine and glasses.

As the winter approached, and we had more time to work on our new house, it soon became apparent that the empty roof space could fairly easily be utilised and had, just about, enough space for a bedroom and bathroom. One of the few negative aspects of the house was that the surviving stone built back wall had been covered on the inside of the house by a very crude timber framed plasterboard skin. This looked very nice, straight, square and clean. The trouble was that, since these old stone walls, over two feet thick were built using larger stones on the outer skin which were held in place with cement and lime mortar but the "cavity" in between was simply filled with small stones and a sort of clay, soil and straw rubble. The problem was that, with time, various forms of small wildlife could get into the walls which provided warmth and shelter for their nests and, ultimately in our case, they got into the gap between the wall and the plasterboard skin so that we had to listen to them rummaging around as though they were wearing hob nail boots. This was very disturbing for Mother and me so I tried making small holes in the plasterboard and pouring mouse poison into the space. To no advantage since dead mice smell very bad! Not a good idea, so the plasterboard had to go and the naked stone wall had to be sealed behind a thick cement render. Stripping back the plasterboard skin wall also meant dismantling my bedroom wall so we decided to fit a staircase in the space and, cutting a hole in the ceiling, get access to the roof space to create a new bedroom. This meant that, by opening the kitchen side wall into the old bedroom space, we could have a much more practical kitchen dining area so that we now had a much more spacious ground floor with my new bedroom in the roof space. All I needed to do now was create a drying area for our laundry by building an open roof between the house and the garage.

CHAPTER TEN

The Wildlife

One aspect of life in our first house at Quemper Guezennec was that, in the early days, when I occasionally became depressed by the difficulties of trying to renovate the house we were living in whilst trying to create a business, I could walk down the road to the river at the bottom of the valley and "chill out" or meditate to clear my mind. It was on these occasions when I first became aware of the wildlife with which we were sharing our beautiful surroundings. We were surrounded by a plethora of wild birds including hawks, kestrels and buzzards living in the forest as well as herons, kingfishers, moorhens, egrets and cormorants living around the rivers. Down in the valley I was also privileged to watch the otters at play along with water voles and, since it was a tidal river, I could watch some very large fish jumping out of the water catching odd flies for their supper.

There was one occasion though when I almost got it wrong, on the walk back up the road to my house when I was confronted by a beautiful wild deer about to cross the road in front of me. It stopped, looked at me and ran off, obviously in a hurry, and whilst I was still taking in the surprise of my "face to face", I saw a group of local hunters about to cross the road at the same point .As a matter of simple reflex, I pointed in the direction of the fast disappearing deer and, just as quickly, realised the stupidity of my action which had put the deer's life in jeopardy. I determined to follow the hunters across the field to stop them but was very relieved to meet them on their way back to the road and, when I asked them what had happened, was told that it was a female deer and they are not allowed to shoot females. PHEW.

It had occurred to me that, moving to Paradise and away from the river, I would miss most of this wildlife but I need not have worried since we had a proliferation of birds, foxes and an occasional deer plus whatever fancied taking shelter in my garage. I had been aware, all winter, of a bird nesting on one of the roof timbers in my garage and it became almost a habit to say hello when I walked into the garage and goodbye when I left, although I don't imagine that they understood me.

The reward for my politeness came one spring morning when, as I approached the garage, I noticed one of the birds sitting on the projecting roof timber, outside of the garage, and apparently shouting into the building through a hole. The bird then flew across the road, sat on an overhead wire and started shouting again, it repeated this performance several times and I was beginning to think there was something wrong, perhaps even an unwanted intruder. Then, to my amazement, a tiny head emerged from the hole and a very young bird jumped out onto the timber and watched a couple more flying displays, from what must have been a parent bird, before making an attempt to emulate its parent. After a lot of flapping and fluttering the baby made it across the road and both the parent bird and I shrieked with delight as we did with the three other first flights which followed.

Having spent my formative years living in the city, I had never experienced such a marvellous yet natural event other than on a David Attenborough television programme and so became much more aware of the privilege of being able to share this country and this life with so many creatures which had been living here long before me..

Easter was approaching and Mother and I were invited to join an English club who were having their Easter lunch at the organiser's home in the nearby village of Squiffiec. We easily found the house only to be told that the lunch was in the yard of the house next door because there was more room there for the buffet and various stalls where they were offering a book exchange along with various other items for sale such as you might find at a car boot sale and including some nice Summer clothes for my mannequin, Marilyn. We met several people for whom we were already doing work as well as some "new faces" so I was pleased to be invited to look at some new work. The organisers of the event, a very pleasant retired couple, had started publishing a news sheet which was very useful so we decided to join their club and offered our support including suggesting using Derek's restaurant for future meetings since the neighbour's yard was not considered to be the best venue for meeting on colder days. We were forever grateful to be able to enjoy and subscribe to the benefits of what is, nowadays, known as networking.

My old friend Bob the builder had also introduced us to another retired couple who lived in Saint Gilles Les Bois in a beautiful house with a garden of around three quarters of an acre with a vegetable patch, several fruit trees and a large lawn area. The double "lean-to" garage had parked in it a lovely old Sunbeam saloon car which Bob and Andrea enjoyed riding around in and, occasionally, attending local vintage car rallies. Having been a vintage car fan in England, Bob maintained his contacts with the English Bentley owner's club and, once per year, invited his friends over to France where they congregated on their lawn and we all enjoyed an afternoon chatting with the owners and listening to the stories and the history of such fine and elegant classic cars.

There were always a few French classic car owners present as well so we were able to compare designs and styles. In addition to Bob and Andrea's annual event, there was the French tour of Brittany meeting which lasted two days and involved the participants touring the area with two hour stopovers in certain popular towns where tourists and locals could look around and admire the diverse collection ranging from engine powered bicycles to lorries and fire engines. Mother enjoyed these events as much as I since she was an impressionable young girl when these cars were the latest thing for eligible young things to be seen in.

Easter was always very popular with the French tourists so there would be several events in our region and, since we were no longer needing to work so hard on our own house, we were free to enjoy some of the qualities which make Brittany so special. One of the Easter events was in nearby Pontrieux where they decided to celebrate the Fete Des Lavoirs. As the river Trieux passed through the centre of the town, the old houses lining the river had, before the invention of washing machines, built small laundry rooms at the bottom of their gardens where they could wash their laundry in the river and these washrooms were known as lavoirs. Most villages, Quemper Guezennec included, would have a single communal washing pool also called a lavoir and these laundry areas would provide a meeting place where the women of the village could do their laundry and exchange gossip at the same time.

The lavoirs in Pontrieux were spread along the river bank and, being privately owned, are comparatively luxurious and, having been carefully renovated, provided an attractive focal point so the decision was taken by the Maire to organise an annual event which would bring the locals together and would attract the early tourists. There is a public car park between the shops and the river which provided an ideal area for the entertainment which usually comprised an odd local artiste with a visiting group of professional singers, usually Irish, along with the obligatory bar and barbeque with meat and sausages provided by my friend Dominique and baguettes supplied by the local baker. There is also, on any public event like this, a creperie. The crepe is a Breton speciality and is basically a pancake spread with jam or chocolate spread, rolled up and eaten "on the move" or one can choose the savoury version, called a gallette which is normally made with wholemeal flour and rolled around some ham or a sausage. Both sweet and savoury crepes are absolutely delicious. On the river there were three or four small boats powered by electrical outboard motors or simply rowed and one could enjoy a short trip down the river and admire the lavoirs which would be decorated with flowers and mannequins in period dress. The whole illuminated with spotlights and multi-coloured floodlights.

The afternoon would be spent wandering around the various craft shops and stalls and the evening ended with a spectacular firework display which would normally be set off before the children went home and the adults got down to some serious drinking. Alcohol, in our region, was never a problem since most village bars would open at around seven thirty in the morning so that the farmers could start their working day at dawn and stop at the bar for "a swift one" before going home for breakfast so it was normal for most locals to be drinking beer or wine all day long in between working sessions. When it came to the evening and time for more serious drinking, they were usually too tired to be aggressive and so became affectionate instead which is very good until you are given a big hug by a stocky farmer who should have taken a shower before going out in the evening!!

My customer base continued to expand as one owner sold up and two more joined and I had been introduced to an owner with a very pretty little cottage hidden away down a twisty lane in an area called Pont Camarel. The house was by the river and backed by a coppice wood, the garden was a pretty wild affair but it was not practical to do much work on it since the section nearest the river was almost permanently flooded and the small lawn area in front of the house sat on a few inches of top soil with the granite rock base standing above the grass in places. Nevertheless, it was nicely sheltered from the weather and free from through traffic, it was also compact and very easy to clean through when preparing for guests and so I enjoyed a good relationship with the owners. There was a stone built store on the end of the house which needed the roof to be re-slated before any use could be made of it so I was asked to remove the old slates, saving any re-usable slates for the rear of the roof, and fit new slates to the front side.

During that summer, an English couple moved into a house only a quarter of a mile downstream and decided that they would set up in competition to my Gite cleaning service so I was very pleased when my client told them that he was planning to remain loyal to me using the old saying "why look at the rest when you already have the best". Nice one.

My only disappointment, that year, was when my German clients decided that they would try the new English couple although my loss was short lived as I was introduced to another German couple with a house near to the village of Squiffiec. They had owned the house for almost twenty years, during which time, they had never actually stayed there since they had undertaken a very long term renovation project which meant completely rebuilding the house inside and, since they wanted the work done using German methods and materials, it was proving more than difficult to find a French artisan who could undertake the work.

They were, however, anxious that the one acre garden should be maintained so as to ensure that the house never looked unused and so, with my ride-on mower and strimmer, I was happy to keep it in order and enjoy the extra revenue.
I also met a couple who had recently bought a house near to Callac and they asked me to do some landscaping around their house to create a car parking area with flower border. They had found a nearby garden centre which was selling old railway sleepers so we had a dozen or so delivered along with several tons of gravel and a roll of underlay material to prevent weeds from growing up through the gravel. The drive to and from Callac took a sizeable chunk out of my working day, the only consolation being that the work was very tiring so, after about five hours work, I was exhausted anyway but the effective earning rate caused me to reluctantly decline their request to

take care of the house on the occasions that it was rented to tourists. Properties in the Callac area were still very cheap so, since the number of houses for renovation in our area was in rapid decline, we were receiving a growing number of enquiries from potential buyers who had seen "bargain" houses for sale in that area.

It should be explained that Northern Brittany is effectively divided into two by the main motorway which passes from east to west between Normandy and Brest so that houses on the north side of the motorway are all within easy reach of the Channel coast whereas those to the south are mainly in farming communities and a much greater distance from the coast. Furthermore, to the western end of the motorway, one is moving into the area called Finistere which tends to be the first to receive inclement weather from the Atlantic and the Bay of Biscay, both areas often reported in the BBC's shipping forecast. As these elements became better recognised by the property seekers, so house prices started to increase in our area quite dramatically making the Cotes D'Armor an increasingly expensive "neck of the woods".

With the ever-developing tourist industry, in our area, there came a very enjoyable increase in "events" along with the revival in more traditional fetes such as the annual village sports day in Poulduran. This tiny village where I had created a client's garden and helped renovate the interior of her house, had once been a busy little fishing port and so part of the annual sports day included various unusual competitions using farming and fishing equipment. One involved a lifting challenge requiring the participant to lift, with one hand only, an iron trailer axle over his head, a feat which took considerable effort in both strength and balance and which appeared to subject some of the competitors to such unusual stress that they needed at least one beer and two cigarettes to aid their recovery.

There was another intriguing competition which involved moving what looked like a wheelbarrow with no wheels, which was laden with increasing amounts of granite stone blocks and dragged along a measured path. Other competitions followed, most of which involved throwing various objects. This all provided great entertainment, the spectators wandering from one competition to another mostly either eating crepes or drinking beer "on the move" and the whole atmosphere was most warm and friendly.

My friend Anna, who had found most of my earlier jobs for me, had sold her house quite early on in my time in France and had bought a much smaller house situated on the busy coastal road in St. Michel En Greve, we had done quite a lot of work inside to make it more comfortable for herself and her husband and she was constantly on the lookout for bargain houses. So much so that she had bought houses for most of her friends and both of her sons so the renovation and garden work kept us both fully occupied to such an extent that poor Mother, who was now in her late seventies, was beginning to tire but, despite my warnings, seemed determined to maintain the workload of a woman of half her age.

I needed to find a plan to slow her down since we had always agreed that Mother would stay with me until her health became a problem when she would return to England where she could be looked after "in her own language". Recognising the symptoms was one of the most difficult situations I had been confronted with thus far and I thought hard and long to find a way to prepare both of us for the inevitable day when she would have to return, possibly within the next year.

We had, at least, more free time during the summer so the visits to local fetes and events were a great help and we were pleased to accept invitations from our friends to join them on their outings. One such trip, organised by our friend Lolita, was to an old mill site near to Treverec where the mill had been made into a restaurant and the surrounding houses made into a museum with one of the houses set out exactly as it would have been when it was used as a farm worker's house. When originally built, the houses had only one room with the beds situated in the two corners of one end of the house next to a large, open fireplace whilst the other end of the room was the kitchen dining area. The beds were usually built-in with stout wooden corner posts supporting a header board and curtains, allowing a measure of privacy whilst, inside the "bedroom", was a very small window just below ceiling level which served as an alarm clock so that, when the sunlight came into view, you knew it was time to get up and start work.

The furniture, whilst very basic, was usually ornate and made of very strong wood, such as oak, lighting was by candles and oil lamps and the robust sink had only one tap. If you were lucky enough to have access to running water that is, otherwise you took your bucket out to the well. Most of the cooking was done over the open fire and the exposed ceiling beams were used for drying herbs and, when appropriate, hanging game such as rabbits and pheasants. The roof space was used for drying and storing grain, crops and firewood and usually accessed from a ladder on the outside of the house. Many of these features were reminiscent of my own house at Quemper Guezennec when I first bought it and I often wondered what the houses must have smelled like with so many things happening in such a small area.

As was normal in a group of six or more such houses, the largest, perhaps the manager's house, had, built onto the end of it, a stone bread oven which, whilst accessed from the outside, shared its chimney with the house to which it was attached. The bread oven on this museum site was fully restored and working so we were able to watch the baker making and baking bread. Quite often, in our area, such a working museum was not only an enjoyable experience for the adults but also used by visiting schools as an educational facility.

CHAPTER ELEVEN

Hello Computers

By the time that I had bought the house in Paradise, my customer base had expanded and moved "up market" to the point where I was being frequently asked if I could be contacted by e-mail and it didn't take much research before I realised that I needed to become involved in the world of computers.

I was born into a generation where only the "well off" people had television and there was only one channel, the B.B.C., so I was somewhat sceptical about having to learn about the modern world of technology and internet communication. A conversation with a retired English resident in our area got me started, or so I thought, and I bought from him his "old" computer which was likely to help me develop an understanding of the wonders of computing. Unfortunately, this machine was so old that it depended entirely on the collection of disc programmes, which I also bought, and it had no capacity or facility for use on the internet but it did at least get me started.

Then my friend Viv offered to give me her old computer and this really set me on to a more useful path since it was an Apple computer and, although it still could not get me onto the internet, I quickly learned how to use it and to work my way around some of the programmes which were built into it. I was especially impressed by the fact that there was a voice facility on the notepad programme which would read my messages back to me.

It was at this point that I decided to step into the Twentieth Century and buy a new computer with which I could communicate with my clients in England. So my friend Tom, who did our plumbing and wiring work, took me to the local suppliers assuring me that, since he used to work for IBM, he would be able to help me select the most appropriate equipment.

I became the proud owner of a new P.C. with a printer and readily equipped to connect to the internet using a telephone line called a "dial up" (whatever that meant) which was provided, at some cost, by France Telecom. My learning curve took another steep incline, not made any easier by the fact that the Windows 98 programme was in French so I had to learn to understand computer jargon in two languages at the same time. Nevertheless, with Tom's help, I was soon "chatting" with clients and please to receive enough extra work, by e-mail, to recover the cost of my investment although, as any newcomer to the world of I.T. will know, the more you undertake to use computers, the more need you have for computer compatible equipment.

The first of these add-ons was a camera so that I could photograph, and send by e-mail, work in progress and completed work which also brought me extra work in terms of addition to and modification of existing work, all thankfully self financing.

The only downside to this wonderful progress was that I had to convert mother's private sitting room into an office and mother had to surrender her privacy and grudgingly accepted that most of my evenings were to be spent in my new hi-tech world.

As a long time fan of photography, I enjoyed the digital camera and the ability to download pictures into the computer and then trim and adjust them so that I could eliminate or emphasise elements of the pictures despite the fact that the first camera had fewer pixels than your average postage stamp. The one consolation of such small capacity pictures was that they could be transmitted to my clients in as little as ten minutes, thanks to the wonder of dial up internet! Nevertheless, my interest was aroused so I bought an appropriate computer programme and revived my love for photography.

One of the better aspects of French life at that time was that the cost of living was lower than in England so I was soon in a position to buy a better camera for, what I considered to be, the more permanent pictures so that when I took mother to look around the chateau De La Roche Jagu, I had two cameras, a bit like your average tourist. Our visit to the chateau was especially interesting since, having worked inside some of the older buildings in Treguier, I had found a new fascination for architecture and the chateau had been built over four hundred years earlier by craftsmen using mostly local materials. It sat firmly on the top of the estuary banks, on the outside of a bend in the river Trieux and had a magnificent viewing gallery where one could look upstream towards Pontrieux and downstream towards Lezardrieux as well as the forest on the opposite bank where Vikki and I had been horse riding and the railway line where mother and I had ridden on the steam train. The chateau yard had the usual gift shop and restaurant although, thankfully, they did not sell alcohol, and the whole was surrounded by beautiful gardens

We could also hear shooting which, I later learned was from a nearby clay pigeon shooting club and I remember smiling when I was told that the French term for clay pigeon shooting is baltrap! Usually, when learning new words or terms in French, I would be able to remember them by finding some English equivalent such as the Breton word for chateau being castel, but baltrap needed no key to help me remember!

Another very pleasant afternoon out was a trip to the coast to the east of Pontrieux where there were several small fishing villages and an especially popular beach called Plage Bonaparte, this beach was a well hidden but frequently visited area which had been used by the French resistance, during the second world war, to smuggle Canadian airmen out of France and there were several plaques in both languages commemorating the courage of all concerned.

The views from the cliffs surrounding the bay at Plage Bonaparte were stunning and my library of pictures was increasing by the day whilst Mother was, without realising it, getting the break she deserved and chance to recover from five years of hard work.

Work, thankfully, continued to find us and, in addition to our gite work, we were getting more garden work which was much easier since I had acquired an impressive collection of machinery. One garden which we had been asked to look after was almost "a bridge too far" however. It belonged to one of Anna's clients, an English dealer in antique furniture who had bought a very splendid manor house near to the coast so that he had somewhere to stay on his frequent trips to France when he would buy French antiques to sell to his English clients. The house itself was in good condition but the garden and orchard covered probably three or four acres and had been neglected over recent years so that there was just a modest lawn in front of the house.

The plan was to recover the land one section at a time and ultimately create an area which could be mowed using the clients ride on mower. It took, ultimately, two summer seasons to clear the land since, each time we cleared one section, another space was revealed and gathering and burning the debris took almost as much time and effort as cutting it down in the first place. Progress became slower with each visit since, before we could start to clear a section, the existing and therefore growing lawn, had to be mowed first. As we cleared each new section, we discovered more about what the manor must have looked like in its hey day with ruined out buildings, remains of barns and gardens and, in addition to the orchard, a range of chestnut, walnut and fig trees so we were able to enjoy autumn treats as the fruits matured. I will always remember the splendour of the house and its impressive grounds but cannot admit to having enjoyed spending six hours riding round in ever decreasing circles cutting the ultimate expanse of grass!

I was determined that, if this was to be Mother's last summer in France, we would make the best of our favourite event in July. Our favourite town of Treguier had, for many years, used its Wednesday market day to celebrate the Breton culture with a music evening every Wednesday in July. As the markets in our area normally closed soon after lunch, it was easy for a number of stall holders to keep their position in the old market square and the commune had erected two covered stages with appropriate lighting, one in the main square and the other in a secondary square linked to the cathedral by a one hundred metre pedestrian street. There were several bars and restaurants facing the cathedral and other shops and restaurants on the street which linked the two squares so the cafes and restaurants lined the pavements with tables and chairs and, by seven o'clock in the evening, the locals and tourists alike, began to gather in anticipation.

By eight o'clock, the scene was set and a local Breton band with various wind instruments, including bag pipes, and percussion section gathered at the top of the Rue Saint Yves and, to a roll of drums, played and marched into the main square. It was like stepping back in time as the band formed into a circle and played their unique Breton tunes whilst the locals and a few adventurous tourists formed a larger circle around the band and danced, hand in hand, around the performers. This shrill but most charming music continued for about half an hour before the flag bearing leader of the group lead the march around the back of the cathedral and left the square open for the visiting performers to light up the two stages and the entertainment continued. Since the Gallic link between Brittany and Ireland is still quite strong, the band in the main square was usually Irish whilst the band in the secondary square would be either French or south American and yet neither effected either since the street linking the two squares did not carry the sound. So whilst the main square had restaurants, bars and cafes with tables where one could enjoy the entertainment and enjoy the market stalls, the secondary square had more basic "fast food" stalls and long tables with bench seating where one could enjoy the normal crepes, gallettes and moules with frites.

The stalls in the main square comprised mostly souvenirs and curios from Africa as well as a variety of unusual sweets and delicacies. One of our favourites was a man who had a stall displaying his collection of buildings and models made entirely from matchsticks, and one was invited to put a few euros into his collection tin as an expression of appreciation of his fine art which must have taken him many hours to assemble. Once the Breton band had dispersed, there would be a variety of "performers" to entertain the children and we were most amused to see, on several occasions, an old London bus parked in the square with a traditional puppet show operated by a young Englishman who toured Brittany every summer and earned a living in much the same way as our guitar playing friend.

The whole event provided a unique entertainment and an atmosphere of congeniality that was enjoyed by all and sundry. By eleven o'clock in the evening, the Breton band gathered up again and the evenings entertainment was rounded off with a final parade and dance leaving the crowds to disperse at their leisure and, it must be said, during all of our visits to these events, we never once saw any drunken or aggressive behaviour that has almost become part of life in most cities in recent times. These most enjoyable events provided not only great entertainment for mother and me but also helped greatly with my meet and greet service.

In the Gites most tourists, when they arrived, were new to the area and had little or no knowledge of where they could visit especially if they had only one week in which to discover Brittany. It was usually helpful if I could point out a few places of interest or recommend forthcoming events. I always felt that it would have been beneficial if the local tourist board had published a monthly newsletter to this effect since local events were rarely publicised and any holiday, as is obvious, can be spoiled by wasting time looking for something to do or see. It must be said, however, that Pontrieux had a very informative tourist information centre unfortunately, it only seemed to be open on a Thursday between two and three in the afternoon unless there was an "R" in the month or you happened to see the manager's bicycle parked outside! Most of "my" tourists, however, seemed to appreciate my half hour presentation when they would ask about which of the thirty five weekly markets were the best to visit or which of the miles of beautiful beaches would best please their family.

Later on that summer, my friend Sven decided to marry his beautiful lady, Heike, so a civil marriage was arranged with the Maire of Pommerit Le Vicomte and Mother and I were invited and I was asked to bring my camera along to be the official photographer. The bride had asked her parents to come along from Germany and, since Sven's parents lived next door to Sven, both Bride and Groom were well supported. As the happy couple were well known to the locals, both the ceremony and the reception at Sven's house were multinational affairs and we had lots of fun switching from one language to another with appropriate translations passing back and forth as necessary. Fortunately, the weather was perfect so both the photographs and following buffet were enjoyed on the patio outside and, needless to say, no-one was seriously drunk just customarily affectionate.

Amongst our new acquaintances since moving into Pommerit, we had met a very pleasant couple with their holiday home on the outskirts of the village which they had owned for over twenty years having done most of the restoration work themselves. The house was beautifully furnished since Mick had an antiques business in England and, as his wife was a teacher, they had plenty of time in France to look after and enjoy their house but it was during the early Spring, when the grass was growing at an alarming pace, that they needed my help. Later that summer, they decided to apply for a permit to build a wall along the front of their house by the roadside so we prepared the foundations together and Mick left me to build the wall and the gate posts during the autumn.
During the same season, the village supermarket was sold to new owners since the previous owner had let the business run down due, in the main part, to there being a problem with alcohol. Quite often, one would have trouble understanding the owner since slurred French is no better than slurred English and there were odd occasions when it seemed as though she couldn't see you well enough to know who she was speaking to anyway !

So we were introduced to Fred and Anya, he being French and Anya being Polish. We were immediately impressed with Fred's shopkeeping and stock control skills and we had to fall in love with the lovely Anya who, in addition to Polish, spoke French and English and did a very good job of looking after their eight year old daughter whilst running their home and working endless hours at the shop.

Another Pommerit resident was my client who had loaned me his motorbike for my afternoon ride with Heike and he had decided to have a swimming pool installed in his garden. He had bought the pool, a five-metre diameter pool, from a local company who had recently opened their business near Lanvollon and had given him a price for installing the half submerged pool and installing the filter pump in his garage. The contractor arrived with his mini-digger and dug an appropriate hole about two metres deep in the centre with a half metre step around the edge, he then built the timber support wall which stood about one metre above ground so that the plastic liner could be fitted as a one piece unit.

The filter pump was connected to the pool, water was introduced and within a couple of days, it was ready for action.

Since I already had experience with pool cleaning, it was easy to add an occasional clean up to my garden servicing schedule and so everything seemed fine. Unfortunately, within a couple of months, the concrete base of the pool underneath the plastic liner developed a crack and one side of the pool began to drop to an extent that put the liner under stress and caused an unsafe step across the bottom of the pool. My client contacted the supplier but was told that responsibility for the foundation was with the contractor who dug the original installation but, when we contacted the contractor, we were told that the installation was the first one he had done and the pool supplier had not given him accurate specifications to work from.

Unfortunately for the pool supplier, my client was not the type of person to be "messed with" in such a way so he asked me to help with translation for a court case to resolve the situation. A very pleasant lady solicitor was recommended to us and we went off to Guingamp to meet her and discuss the appropriate procedure. I suspect that the pool supplier was not used to such resolute action because suitable compensation was negotiated and, thankfully, neither my client nor I had to appear in court.

Soon afterwards, Mother and I were invited to join him, his family and friends to a Pig Roast which he wanted to have in his garden to thank his neighbours for their support and "christen" his new pool. This was a truly great event since a number of the older neighbours had enjoyed this type of traditional event as young men and they were able to find and assemble a large roasting spit which was lit mid-morning so that, by mid-day, it was hot enough for them to be able to put the small pig onto the spit and a four hour roast was under way!

By the time Mother and I arrived, just before six in the evening, the tables were set, the lights were switched on and the "working party", having laboured for several hours over the hot roast whilst consuming copious amounts of beer and wine, was beginning to get a little boisterous, one might say. The atmosphere was magic with thirty or more people, English, French, Polish, and German, chattering and laughing with the excited anticipation of tasting the roasted pig which had been turned and basted for several hours with an aromatic mixture of herbs and oils, the recipe known only by the aforesaid working party.

After that summer season, my client, of several years, with her part-finished development in Plouec Du Trieux had decided to sell her property and move on and asked me to try to find her a buyer so I approached my client with the broken swimming pool who was looking for investment opportunities. This seemed too good an opportunity to miss and I took him to look at the property which, by now, still had only two working Gites but there were two more almost finished with a fifth Gite still to be done. My client, being a shrewd businessman, made an offer which would have recovered her costs and given her a small profit but, try as I might, I could not persuade her to accept so I reluctantly passed the message on only to be told that, had the sale been successful, my commission for the work would have been the gift of his beautiful BMW motorbike! This situation is known in the trade as "Sod's Law".

During that Summer season, Brittany we were told, was to provide a stage of the Tour De France cycle race and that part of the route would involve them passing through the centre of Pontrieux! This was another of those opportunities not to be missed so, on the appointed day, Mother and I drove up to Pontireux and found a viewing point where we were sure to see the event. There were already a hundred or so people lining the roadside when we arrived which was quite a crowd for Pontrieux and, only half an hour later, the first course clearing cars passed through with lights flashing and motorbike mounted Gendarmes flanking them with sirens singing.

Excitement was building and more spectators were arriving as the publicity cars came through the town followed by more Gendarmes, more publicity cars and so on for almost an hour. Mother was running out of patience as the first motorbike marshals arrived and she turned to me and asked how much longer we would have to wait. As she turned to me, there was a shriek from the crowd, a loud whooshing sound which lasted all of two minutes and.... that was it!! We decided that it would probably be better to watch it on television in the future.

There were two bars in the nearby village of Saint Clet, where I had put new slates on a house roof. One was a tabac/bar since cigarettes and tobacco were not sold in any other shops in France and all prices were fixed so there was no question of saving money by buying in bulk or hoping to save money at a supermarket. This system works well and provides a meeting point for locals to exchange news, views and gossip whilst picking up some cigarettes or a newspaper.

The tabac in Saint Clet was run by a family whose father and son worked as electrician and plumber whilst the mother ran the shop. I had asked Herve and his son to help me to get electricity connected to the house at Quemper Guezennec and well remember the day when Herve left his son at my house to fit a fuse box, with power points, to the wall by the meter. We were less than impressed when the son opened his tool box, took out his electric drill and asked where the nearest power point was so that he could drill the holes to mount the fuse box!

He failed to see the funny side when I told him that it would probably be in the house next door, a hundred or so yards down the road!! So we had to sit and make polite conversation with him until his father arrived to take him home for lunch when, needless to say, some less polite words were exchanged between father and son and they had to come back in the afternoon with appropriate hand tools.

The other bar in St. Clet was a restaurant which was run by a robust but attractive single lady who would keep the bar open until the small hours in the morning or as long as there were people spending money. This was, of course, against the law but, when the Gendarmes called in to check, they would simply be offered a free beer and invited to join in with whatever subject was being discussed. The lady owner took a shine to my friend Bob the builder and, since his wife was temporarily back in England, and we both enjoyed Marie T's company, we would often spend an hour at her bar at the end of a day's work.

The only trouble was that Bob didn't speak French and Marie T didn't speak English so I had to sit between them and translate which, as I pointed out to Bob, depended on me telling him what she had really said and my not mentioning our chats to his wife!

Most of the larger villages would have a restaurant, and Marie T's was no exception, where local artisans would go for their two hour lunch break and these restaurants would offer their "Menu Ouvrier" which would comprise a three course meal of soup, main course and dessert for around seven pounds. This was fantastically good value and it was universally accepted that there would be a menu of the day with no variations but there was always more than enough food and it would be well cooked. Another coincidental advantage was that one always knew when it was mid-day since there would be large groups of parked lorries and white vans jamming the centre of the villages which had restaurants.

My fiftieth birthday was rapidly approaching and Mother was concerned that she would not be able to make it into the significant celebration that should be enjoyed when reaching "the half century" but, as the day approached, I started to receive lots of birthday cards from friends and family in England as well as clients and friends in France.

The day dawned and I had decided to take the day off from my work and was wondering whether to take Mother out for a menu ouvrier lunch when Bob the builder telephoned to tell me to keep the evening free. To my delight, a group of friends had organised a celebration for me at Marie T's restaurant where a room had been reserved and a meal organised with birthday cake and party hats! I was surprised, delighted and almost overwhelmed by the friendship and affection of that evening which I shall never forget and, thank goodness, a set of photographs which I shall always treasure.

CHAPTER TWELVE

The End Of Mother's Adventure

One of the reasons that Mother had agreed that she would stay with me in France, for as long as her health permitted, was that she didn't speak French so I would have to be with her to translate and, whilst that was not a problem, there could be no dignity for Mother or privacy for her if I had to explain to a doctor what ails an old woman. I had already learned this when I was asked to accompany my friend Bob the builder whilst he was examined in some private parts by the local doctor.

There was also the problem that France does not have a National Health Service, as in England, so one has to have private medical insurance which is expensive and, like other insurances, is paid retrospectively. I experienced this quite early on when I needed dental treatment and had to pay on the day of the treatment but only received seventy five per cent reimbursement from the insurance company which did not impress me especially since the dentist was almost brutal in his treatment methods. I had also decided to visit the local doctor to ask whether anything could be done to help control a tremble which I had suffered since my motorbike racing days. The doctor took my blood pressure, asked me whether any members of my family had Parkinson's Disease, told me the tremble would get worse and took ten pounds cash from me. Say no more.

As our season drew to a close, Mother finally admitted that raking up hedge clippings and helping mix cement was becoming too much and her legs were starting to cause her discomfort. I mentioned the problem to my daughter Philippa and asked her to help me find somewhere for Mother to live back in England. By November, Philippa was working in a care home and she telephoned me to say that there was a place available for Mother in the home where she worked.

I needed to see the home before applying so I got a lift to the ferry port at Roscoff and a coach to Derby which was my first crossing without a car. The ferry arrived in Plymouth at seven o'clock in the evening so Philippa had booked a ticket for me on the eight thirty coach to Derby so I found the coach station and waited..... and waited....and waited. The coach finally arrived at ten o'clock and my situation got no better when the coach driver politely informed me that the Derby coach didn't leave until eight thirty in the morning! Clearly, we were meant to book a coach using a twenty-four hour clock. I managed to persuade the driver to take me to London where I could change onto a coach for Derby but that didn't arrive at Derby until fourteen hundred hours the next day!

Finally, I arrived in Derby and went directly to the residential home where Philippa was working and was given the guided tour. The home was very pleasant and quite clean but I could not visualise Mother being "dumped" after the life she had enjoyed in recent years especially when I realised that the residents were, in the main, older and much less active than Mother. I concluded that it would not be a good idea to pursue Mother's application any further and Philippa took me to her house where I would spend the night before going back to France.

We had also discussed the fact that Philippa and Duncan had decided to sell their Ford Escort in favour of a larger car to accommodate their daughter, Taylor, and the toys, pushchair and other paraphernalia so I made them an offer they couldn't refuse and, instead of going back to France on a coach, booked a ferry ticket for me and a car and off I went.

Having spent the last four years driving left hand drive cars, it was a little strange getting used to changing gear with my left hand although most other controls were in the same place. The other difference was that Philippa's car was petrol powered so I had to take care to put the correct fuel in but I did find it easier driving on the left hand side of the road in a right hand drive car, until, that is, I drove off of the ferry in France!!

Mother was a little confused when I arrived back in France with another car but I explained that my Renault estate was getting rather tired and, since the Escort had almost twelve months road tax and M.O.T., it was a cheap way of keeping things going for a while. I am not sure how she felt about my report on the home I had visited since she was beginning to adjust to the idea of retiring back to England where my sister, daughters and other family all lived but she did agree that it was too early in life for her to stop altogether.

On one of our regular visits to Derek's restaurant in Pommerit, Mother was expressing her regrets about going back to England and saying how much she would miss the beautiful countryside when Derek suggested we borrow his video camera and make a film about the area and our favourite spots so that she would have something to show friends and family when she finally went back.

This was a great idea so we set off on Christmas day in the morning to do a tour of the area arriving back in Pommerit by dark when the very pretty Christmas lights were showing our village in a different but equally colourful light. I gave the camera back to Derek the following day, having also filmed inside our house at Paradise and he edited the film and was proud to present Mother with a half hour souvenir film which she treasures and watches with a tear in her eyes. We had taken our tour in the French Renault since Mother had registered her dislike of the English Escort car because, being right hand drive, it meant that she, as the passenger, was sitting in the middle of the road as we drove along so on-coming traffic was uncomfortably close to her.

On Monday of the last week of January, Philippa telephoned from England.

"Hi dad, I've got good news and bad news, which do you want first?"

"We need some good news" I replied.

"Well I've found somewhere for Grandma to live and it is really good. I went to see it today, it is a one bedroomed flat in a quiet square comprising around thirty flats reserved for people over sixty years old. There is a resident warden who is available twenty four hours and a community room where they have meetings two or three times per week for the residents and it is on the edge of a fairly new estate with open countryside beyond."

"That sounds perfect" I couldn't hide the excitement in my voice "So what's the bad news?"

"We have to get her in by the end of the week!"

I was reminded of an American saying about something unpleasant hitting the fan. The conversation went on about the flat and the area and, since it was only two miles from where Philippa lived, she would be able to visit Mother regularly although, with the warden calling twice a day, there should be no problems about caring for Mother and, since all of the neighbours were of retirement age, there were unlikely to be too many problems with late parties or drunken behaviour.

I put the telephone down and my mind was thrust into a state of near panic. How on Earth was I going to organise Mother's return within the four days available? The fact that we were at the end of January meant that there was no problem in taking time off work so I began, as I usually do, by making a list of jobs to do and their priorities. Numbers one and two had to be organising transport and booking the ferry so I asked a few friends and was directed to a Europe-wide hire company in Guingamp where I booked the largest van I could afford and then booked the ferry. Next on the list was to sort the minimum amount of furniture which would have to include Mother's most treasured items such as her antique china cabinet, bar, wardrobe and dressing table all of which she had owned for many years and shared with my Father. Then we needed to pack her belongings which, she insisted, would have to include my collection of trophies which I had won in my motorcycle racing days along with her collection of miniature and ornamental wine bottles, which she had first started to collect in the late nineteen fifties. By Tuesday evening, we had gathered so many items that there would be no space in the van for her bed but she wasn't bothered since it was already well past its sell by date. So I went to the hire company on Wednesday morning and collected the van so that we could start, by lunchtime, to load Mother's belongings ready for an early start on Thursday. We sat, exhausted, to eat dinner on Wednesday evening and the realisation hit her, like a slap in the face, that her great adventure was over and she would be setting sail, the next day, back to England to retire peacefully and reflect on the many exciting years she had seen since World War Two. Culminating with six extraordinary years in France. She started to cry and there was no point in trying to console her.

"I know it's not going to be easy but you will still have your independence, your medical needs will be properly attended to and you will soon settle down and find new friends with Philippa only five minutes away." I gave her a hug. "Shut up." she replied.

We had to be at St.Malo by nine thirty in the morning so we got up early and Mother had one last look around before climbing into the van and we were under way. Most of the journey was spent with Mother reminiscing about her great adventure and the people we had met and it wasn't until we drove off of the ferry and onto England's crowded motorway that she started to think about our destination and what she might be expecting.
The flat was owned by Derby Council and Philippa and Vicky had worked hard, once they got access to the flat, to make it comfortable for Mother so that she would be able to sleep there as soon as we arrived, all we had to do was get her furniture installed. We arrived by ten thirty that evening and were instantly impressed with the size and layout of the flat and especially grateful that the girls had been able to get carpets for the living room and bedroom as well as a bed so we had a cup of tea and left Mother to settle down to her first night back in England.

I went to the flat the next morning, having spent the night at Philippa's house, and we struggled to move the furniture from the van into the flat since it was on the first floor so everything had to be carried upstairs. When everything was in, it looked really nice and we were satisfied that Mother would be safe and comfortable especially as the warden came in to introduce himself and see that Mother had everything that she needed. The only thing that she was worried about was that, for the first time in several years, she would be alone and we could only imagine what emotions she went through as I said goodbye and set off back to France.
The girls promised to get her a telephone as soon as possible so that Mother could speak to me regularly and assured us both that all would be well.

I arrived at my house in Paradise on Sunday and was absolutely exhausted so I cooked something to eat, opened a bottle of wine, slumped into my chair in front of the television and then it hit me........Silence, Total Silence.

Since the break-up of my marriage, some sixteen years earlier, I had spent the first six years living alone and, since then, had lived with Mother so the sudden absence and consequent silence was something that would take time for me to adjust to. Nevertheless, I had plenty of work available to me and it would take me until the end of February to catch up with the backlog of work which had built up through December and January.
My Gite cleaning business had now grown to twelve and I had enquiries for another three Gites to begin after Easter so I was going to have to look for help on Saturdays, at least, when there could be as many as six exchanges to deal with on the one day.

Fortunately, my friend whose barn I had helped to convert into a Gite in the early days, had two daughters and the older girl Lydia had completed her secondary education in France and taken a course at Manchester University. This meant that she would be spending the long summer holiday in France and offered to help me with the Gites. The idea of working with Lydia was going to be fun since, apart from her obvious beauty, she was great fun to be with, extremely intelligent and keen to maintain the high standard of cleanliness which I had built my business on.

Since Lydia wasn't due to arrive until July, my early season was going to be hectic since most of the Gites needed their gardens to be serviced but I had all of March to get the first cuts, strimming and pruning done so everything was ready for Easter.

The English club, which I had joined, had booked their Easter lunch at Derek's restaurant in Pommerit and, naturally, I attended as a member but there were over forty visitors so Derek asked me if I could help with the catering as a support to their table staff. I was, of course, pleased to assist but my first function was to serve the wine, this was not a good idea since I had a rather unpleasant tremble which meant that, even using two hands, I was spilling wine over the table cloths as I missed the wine glasses and the diners were not impressed. Of the many "careers" I have attempted during my many working years, my time as a wine waiter was by far the shortest having lasted for no more than half an hour although, being made redundant and advised to join my fellow diners, was much more fun.

Having lived for two years in her smaller house at St.Clet, Lolita decided it was time to move on and found an even smaller renovation project, near to her artist friend, only a couple of miles from Callac. The house itself was quite small with only one bedroom in the roof space but Lolita soon had a plan to convert the old forge into a utility room with staircase into the roof space which would give her the extra space for two more bedrooms. The artist friend had lived in her house for a couple of years and recommended a local, English, builder to do the structural work since our friend Bob the builder had returned to England to open a pub and restaurant in the South West of England so I was invited to work with the new builder.

With the news of Lolita's pending move, an English couple, for whom I had done some work in the early days, decided to hold a party in Lolita's house in St.Clet. Their house, though quite splendid, was in the centre of Pontrieux which meant that parking would be difficult and, since the Gendarmerie was not far away, drinking and driving would be somewhat risky so the idea of partying in open countryside was best and any late noise problems were eased by inviting Lolita's neighbours to join us.

The party began, in the usual way, with drinks in the house and it wasn't long before there were twenty or thirty people gathered and, as there were some smokers in the congregation, we separated into groups so as not to interfere with the food preparation. After about half an hour of chatter, I was approached by the lady organiser and invited to follow her towards the end of Lolita's house furthest from the kitchen so I picked up my wine glass and followed obediently thinking she might want to discuss work but was taken off guard a little when she took me outside and pointed to a wooden bench seat by the side of the house.

"We put that there so that you could sit outside when you are smoking your cigarettes." She said in a matter of fact way and went back inside without another word.

I was shocked, at first, then angry at being treated in such an off hand manner this was, after all, France where smokers were still in the majority and furthermore I had asked Lolita about smoking in her house and she had no objections so long as I didn't smoke in the kitchen.

I sat on the bench and boiled whilst I finished my glass of wine then got into my car and drove home. I had just poured my second glass of wine when my telephone rang. Hi, Lolita here, why did you go home?"

"I was told that I must go outside to smoke in your house despite having previously asked for your permission to smoke inside so I went home where I don't have to ask anybody about where I should go to smoke". I was, perhaps, a little blunt with Lolita whose friendship I did not want to jeopardise.

There followed a brief conversation with Lolita which gave me chance to repair the damage of my response and then the lady organiser came to the `phone and justified her judgement but "insisted" that I should go back to the party. I refused and never spoke to the lady again but was grateful that Lolita acknowledged my point so our friendship was not damaged. Was this, I wondered, my first experience of "grumpy old manhood"?

Work was still going well and my client with the house in Goudelin had decided that the time had come to do something with his building plot in the centre of the village so he sent me an outline plan and asked me to organise a building permit. I had learned, from previous experience, that the easiest way to achieve any such permit was to get a local architect to do the plans and then submit on our behalf the plans to the DDE (planning authority) and then to the local Maire, who he probably knew. The plans were prepared and submitted but the Maire was not very keen on the idea of having two houses and a swimming pool in the village centre and several other councillors objected as well so the permit was denied which left my client with something of a white elephant since he was not prepared to reduce his ambition. He was further angered when one of the councillors offered to buy the land at a "knock down price" (food for thought).

As the holiday season was about to start, I had a call from my friend Dominique to ask me if I wanted to buy another goat but I was a little reluctant after my earlier experience with the lesbian goat. Nevertheless, he persisted insisting that this goat was already pregnant and, since it was a rare breed, I would be able to sell the kid when it came of age, recoup my cost and still be able to enjoy the mother with her milk. I accepted the offer and took delivery of a beautiful, bulging goat who was very friendly, having been a family pet, so I cleared the covered area between the garage and the house and laid a straw bed in readiness for the pending birth. Only one week later, just as the goat and I were getting to know each other, I was woken at four in the morning by the goat who was kicking up an awful din. Since it was dark and I was in no position to investigate the noise, I turned over and went back to sleep. The next morning I went to make sure that the goat hadn't been eaten by a fox and, to my astonishment, was met by a beautiful baby goat who had, apparently, just struggled to its feet and mother who was looking a little sore but obviously proud.

Since Mother's return to England, I had telephoned her every day with my news so she was as pleased as I was to learn about my new arrival and made me promise to send her some photographs as soon as I could. Happily, for me, both goat and kid were in perfect condition with no apparent problems so I telephoned Dominique to tell him and ask him what I needed to do next in terms of protecting them and how I should make sure that the baby didn't wander off in the night. I was assured that it was enough to keep the mother tied on to a twenty foot tether because the baby would not leave its mother's side for a couple of months. Nevertheless, I put chicken wire ends to the covered area to secure them at night and put the mother onto her tether during the day to make sure that they would both be there when I got home from work.

This system worked well for several weeks and the kid grew very quickly and began to become a little adventurous to the point where I stepped outside one morning to get ready for work and didn't see the kid with its mother as it usually would be. Just as I was about to worry, I found it, fast asleep, on the roof of my car!
"Have you seen where your baby is?" I asked the goat "what kind of mother are you?" She didn't answer so I applied myself to the kid.
"You can't stay there, I need to go to work and you need to go to your mum for breakfast." I was ignored.
I decided to carry on regardless and load the car with my gardening machinery ready for work but the kid didn't move so I went back indoors for a last coffee before setting off. Half an hour later it was still there, just out of my reach, so I decided that, once I started the engine, it was bound to jump up and run back to its mother. Wrong again. The only thing left was to roll the car forwards since it, surely, would get the message but I was getting nowhere so I put the brakes on and sat and watched as the kid slid down the windscreen, along the bonnet and landed, with surprising grace, on all four feet at the front of the car. I speak English and French but not Goat so I didn't understand what the kid shouted at me before it strode arrogantly off back to its mother although the mother's expression, as she glared at my car, suggested that they both thought that I had done the wrong thing. The kid continued to sleep on the roof

of my car, especially on nice sunny days, but knew that if I opened the car door, it was time to get off!

Having two cars for the Summer proved to be very useful since I could have my gardening and building tools in the Renault estate and the gite cleaning equipment in the Ford escort so I could use the appropriate car for my work. This was particularly helpful that Summer as I had fifteen gites to look after so I was particularly grateful that Lydia was there to help me and she was pleased to have a clean, cement dust free car to ride in although it was sometimes confusing if I had to drive both left hand drive and right hand drive cars on the same day.

Mother had settled well into her new flat in Derby and the resident warden was taking especially good care of her whilst my daughter Philippa called in every two or three days so my daily telephone calls were mostly made up of chat about the new neighbours. I was pleased that she didn't seem to be too unhappy about leaving France but she sometimes expressed concern about my reports on the Gite cleaning work which reached its peak in mid-August when Lydia and I cleaned and exchanged ten Gites in one day. So my summer season passed by in a haze of work and trips to Callac to help finish the renovation of Lolita's new house which she wanted to move in to before October.

My work was developing to the point where, as my reputation grew, new clients were calling me on an almost regular basis so I used the Summer evenings in Treguier as a meeting point so that we could discuss whatever project was on offer in a relaxed atmosphere, besides which, it usually meant that I was provided with a glass or two of wine to help things along.

During that Summer my client, whose house we had renovated with two and a half thousand floor tiles, decided he wanted a house by the sea so he registered his first house with Brittany Ferries so that it could be rented out as a Gite and found a very pleasant house overlooking the port at Brehec. The house was in a superb location and was not more than fifty years old so there were none of the problems with dampness normally expected with older, stone built houses and it had belonged to a retired couple who had fitted the house with all manner of modern gadgetry. The only problem was that the gadgets had been modern twenty years earlier but were, by now, somewhat worn and in an almost dangerous condition so the first job was to rewire and make safe inside the house whilst the well cared for garden was easy to re-arrange.

The original owners of the house had decided, upon their retirement, to divide the half acre of land into four plots and had sold the house and two plots of the land whilst retaining the area closest to the road where they had built a new house for themselves. New houses were built on the remaining plots but, since the land sloped down towards the bay, each of the houses enjoyed a view out to sea and my client's house enjoyed a spacious verandah accessed from the lounge and big enough for family barbeques.

Since my client worked in the construction industry in England, he determined from the onset that the existing bedroom with bathroom in the roof space could easily be adapted to provide two further bedrooms so his new retired neighbours introduced him to the English architect/builder who had built their house and whose office was only two hundred yards down the road. In no time at all, permits had been granted and work had started on the improvements so I stayed out of their way for most of that autumn.

As so often happened, on these occasions, I was about to have a few weeks of easy going on the work schedule when I was invited to dinner with a client for whom I had created a bathroom. He explained to me that one of his wife's work colleagues had bought a house near to Limoges in the Massif Central region and wanted some help to renovate it but, since my friend Bob the builder was back in England, I needed the help of another builder because I was not prepared to undertake structural work myself. My friend Anna suggested that her builder, Steve, and I should work together so the house owner booked a gite near to the house where Steve and I would meet up with three other men who were going to clear some of the trees surrounding the house. It never ceases to surprise me how big the country of France is so, despite setting off at nine in the morning, we didn't find our gite until seven in the evening and all we achieved on route was to find the nearest supermarket and builder's merchant. Our tree-felling colleagues arrived two hours later so, at least, Steve and I had time to choose the best bedrooms and to find out how to make the television work.

We set off the next morning, with our map and directions, to find the house which was described as being ten minutes away but we were never able to do the journey in less than half an hour. The house had obviously been abandoned several years earlier and was in a very poor condition, Steve and I looked at each other and tried not to say anything unpleasant about it that might be reported back to the owners. Our initial task was to remove the slates so that the roof could be replaced and the house rendered weather proof but it took us two days, with the help of the tree fellers, to clear the wood and vegetation around the house and give us enough space to erect our scaffold tower. Once the tower was in place, Steve made a start on the old slates and instructed me to clear out the inside of the house so that we could store any re-usable slates downstairs and then work on the roof timbers from inside the house.
It was evident that there had been squatters in the main part of the house but, apparently, not for several years so the mess and smell made progress very difficult although one could imagine that it had once been a lovely house situated half way up a large hill and surrounded by natural forest.Our tree-felling colleagues were soon

busy with their chain saws and were obviously very skilled as they cut down several trees, which had grown within a matter of feet from the house, without ever risking damage to us or the house. The men with the chain saws were not impressed with the location of the house, describing it as being MFN (middle of f*****g nowhere), so there was nothing to do in the evenings except drink wine and watch French television which is not an exciting experience if you are used to a choice of twenty or more channels. So the tendency was to spend the main part of the day working arriving back at the gite by dark.

As a result of the longer hours, we had the roof stripped and re-usable slates stored by the end of the first week so I continued clearing the inside of the house whilst Steve started securing the doors, windows and sealing the tops of the exposed walls with cement. At one end of the house was a small and dilapidated old extension with a traditional bread oven the roof of which had collapsed.
This, I found, was very interesting since it gave us a chance to see how these ovens were constructed and we were able to work out that the brick built dome of the oven would have been supported, during its construction, by an internal timber frame. When built, the timber frame was then removed leaving the dome, with chimney, self-supporting. Unfortunately, since the dome had long since collapsed, there was a lot of rubble inside the oven and it had fallen into the bakery area but, as I cleared the bricks and cement, I found a fascinating collection of original bakery pots, pans and even an old wooden spatula which would have been used for moving the bread into and out of the oven. I also found some old newspapers which disintegrated as soon as I picked them up but at the bottom of the heap, I found a hand written diary dated 1913! I took the liberty of keeping the spatula and the diary as souvenirs.

Once I had cleared the inside of the house, Steve asked me to put up the scaffold at the other end of the house to clear the pinion wall of ivy which had completely covered the wall. This plant can be very attractive but must be controlled so, when the house was abandoned, the ivy took over. Since these old stone built houses consist mainly of a faced stone inner and outer wall with clay, rubble and dust in between, once the roof starts to leak, the water gets into the wall and provides nutrition for the ivy so that the ivy sends roots into the wall. This dislodges the stones to an extent that can deform the wall and cause it to become unstable. As soon as I revealed the problem, I called for Steve to come and examine the situation so it was decided not to remove any more ivy but to cut it from ground level so that it would be less likely to grow with such aggression until the client arrived and a decision could be taken on progress for the future.

By the end of our two weeks, everything had been cleared and the house actually looked rather nice nestled, as it was, in the forest so when the client arrived and we departed on the same day, it was a case of offering first the good news and then the bad news. During my time in France, I experienced, on many occasions, where someone had

81

bought a house without the necessary knowledge or experience to recognise hidden problems such as the one with this house and, what looked like a bargain at the time, could very quickly turn into a burden. My sympathy for clients on the occasions never diminished.

I was told, some weeks later, that the client had suspended his project but would be likely to resume once the necessary finances were arranged.

By the time I arrived back at home, the builders had done their work at Brehec so I was invited to help complete the loft conversion by creating some plasterboard lined storage spaces and other finishing touches so that, when the client arrived with his family for their final holiday of the year, they were able to use the bedrooms upstairs and convert the smaller downstairs bedroom into a games room and study.

This brought me nicely to Christmas and my first opportunity to go back to England for a couple of weeks to be with Mother. Things had gone well for Mother since her return and my daughters, along with the Warden's support, had kept her occupied so that, by the time I arrived, she was well rested and recovered from her hard work in France. We spent the first few days of my visit chatting about people and events in France so we were able to enjoy the week between Christmas and New Year's Day visiting family and friends, some of whom we hadn't seen since we first went to France.

I returned to France in the New Year and got off to a steady start since, although there was still plenty of work on offer, I was moving towards the position of being able to make my own decisions on what to do and when. The remainder of my winter was spent doing smaller, simpler projects for existing owners so that, by the easter start to lettings, everything was ready and all of my gardens were neat and tidy. It was during the week before easter that I was introduced to the son of my accountant client with the house near Treverec. I was very sad to learn that his Father had recently died in his sleep which, although something of a shock, was almost to be expected since he was ninety years old and working to his very last day.

The son and his wife had come to clear the house of personal items and asked me to help find an appropriate Agence Immobilier who would sell the house for them and my final fee would be the small caravan which they had used once per year for their easter family reunion. I accepted with the thought of, perhaps, selling it on to a future owner who might want somewhere to sleep during a renovation and towed it to my house where it could sit on my lawn, by the garage, until I needed it.

It was during my free time after easter that my friends Derek and Sally told me about their plan for the future. They had been in France for some twelve years since buying the restaurant in Pommerit and had worked incredibly hard to restore the business to its earlier level by taking on a contract with a local events organiser to do the catering for weddings and other events which he had organised. This involved preparing meals for parties of between fifty and two hundred guest, delivering to whatever venue had been organised and providing service staff for the event which often meant them achieving only a few hours sleep over an entire weekend so, although financially successful, they were reaching the time when retirement was becoming a very attractive possibility.

They had, as a result of a family bereavement, inherited a modest amount of money and had bought an abandoned old house just south of Brest which they planned to renovate over a two year period so that they could sell their restaurant and retire to what was effectively the other end of Brittany. I was invited to go with them to have a look at their house and consider a plan for renovating it. The journey there took a couple of hours driving through Finisterre then turning south towards the Bay of Biscay and I remember thinking that, whilst they might enjoy the peace and quiet of their new residence, it would not be long before they started to miss the beauty of the Cotes D`Armor which they were proposing to abandon. Nevertheless, the house was very pleasant and one could visualise that it would not take a great deal of work to make it into a comfortable home. The house had obviously been the home of the local blacksmith and farrier since it had a large, brick built forge built to one end of the house with a very small vegetable garden at the other end so providing Sally with some ground for her garden and extra space for her pets whilst Derek could tidy up the forge to provide himself with a workshop and to create a small studio so that their son could pursue his pop music recording ambition.

Whilst Derek had already started the internal renovation, he suggested on the drive back home that I might be able to "do something" with the forge during my quiet period before the Summer rush so we devised a plan and, once back in my house in Paradise, I began to prepare for the work offered. I had three weeks before my season got under way so I decided that, if I set off on a tuesday morning, I could arrive at the house and get three days work done on the house before returning home on thursday evening and would, therefore, only have to sleep in the house for two nights per week.

I loaded my car and trailer with tools and equipment on the monday evening and decided to take with me some of the other domestic essentials so that I would be as near to being self sufficient as possible and set off early on tuesday so that I could reasonably expect to start work before lunch time. I arrived in good time and proceeded to prepare for the work but decided to have a look at my temporary residence during lunch.

There was, inside the house, one useable room upstairs with a couple of beds and a room downstairs with what an English estate agent would describe as a functional kitchen with bathroom off although I would beg to differ and decided to take a sleeping bag, portable gas ring and my own pots, pans and cutlery. My project was to clear the old forge of its machinery and other rubbish, level off the earth floor and lay a six inch thick steel re-enforced concrete floor using materials which I would buy from the local builders merchant some twenty miles away. I determined that, if I worked tuesday, wednesday and thursday, I need spend only two nights sleeping in the house and would have my weekends free to deal with any work required by my other clients and assumed that two weeks should see the job done.

I arrived, on day one, full of enthusiasm and quickly set up camp and unpacked my tools and equipment, including my concrete mixer, so that my trailer would be free to collect the building materials. Things went downhill form there as I found that the uneven earth floor in the forge was actually concealing many years of changes and modifications which meant digging out great lumps of old iron, concrete and bricks which needed to be broken up to provide a foundation and fill in several large holes in the ground before the concrete floor could be laid.

At the end of my first tiring day, I went to the shop and bar only a couple of hundred yards away to buy some cigarettes and food for the evening and was pleased but not surprised to be greeted sympathetically by the proprietor who knew something of the history of the house I was about to start work in. I got back to the house to try to relax for the evening and things carried on with their downhill progress when I discovered that the shower didn`t work, the toilet didn't flush properly, there was no light in the bathroom and neither the cooker nor the water heater worked. Just to add to the misery of my exhaustion, I couldn't even find the BBC on my battery powered radio! Never mind, I had my own gas ring, pots and pans so I ate well and took my sleeping bag and a bottle of wine upstairs and settled down with the last of my unanswered questions, how many of God's little creatures was I sharing my bijou accommodation with?

On the third day of my work, I had been asked to go to a nearby village to meet an English couple who had some plans for me to take back to my friend Derek so I finished early and made the modest detour to meet them. The husband was an architect and Derek had asked him to prepare plans for the extension and improvement of his hotel in Pommerit. Evidently he was intending to improve the hotel and restaurant facilities to realise the full value of his property before selling the business. The plan was quite complex and was obviously going to take some time to complete but I decided to "mind my own business" and stick with the task at hand.

By the time I arrived back at my house in Paradise, I was very tired and a little less enthusiastic about the work I still had to do to convert the old forge as it was obviously going to take longer than anticipated. Nevertheless, I was determined to keep to my three week schedule since I had other clients waiting for their pre-season preparations to be dealt with so I was relieved to reach the end of my floor laying work and secretly hopeful that I would not be asked to go back.

With the new season looming, the owners of the block of four gites at Pommerit had arrived to do their own preparation work. This was always an entertaining time for me since one of the owners was an administrative type of person and he would usually want to introduce some new systems for me to operate to help reduce the theft of cutlery, ashtrays, etc. Conversely, the other owner would be busy fitting new floor tiles or restyling one of the bathrooms and since he was a "qualified" builder, having served his apprenticeship with the well known house builders "Bodgit and Scarper", it never failed to amuse me to see how accurate his training had been. They had, however, decided that this would be their final season with the gites and would be looking for a potential buyer so the argument started early on as to whether they would advertise the business on the internet or in the local newspaper. The irony of David's boast about his building industry apprenticeship was that he applied the same philosophy to the work he did on his own property so, whenever he did any work on the gites, I would inevitably be called in by the tourists to repair some of the work he had done only a few weeks earlier. Fortunately, the swimming pool they had installed two years earlier had worked well and was still in place although one was naturally inclined to be a little nervous.

The summer season, that year, passed by almost crisis free and, with Lydia's help, we coped very well and the extra gardening work meant that I could afford to buy a nice new ride-on mower which, unfortunately, didn't fit on to my trailer. Fortunately, for me, my friend Jack decided that he no longer needed his trailer and, since it had a demountable roof, it was ideal for my work. I had known Jack and his wife Mary since my first Winter in France when I had been asked by Bob the builder to do some labouring for him on their house in St. Gilles Les Bois and, with Mary being English, we had become good friends. Being French by birth, Jack had worked in several countries as a young man so Mary and their two children were pleased when Jack decided to "settle down" in his homeland where he bought a restaurant in the beautiful fishing port at Paimpol. The restaurant, though small, enjoyed a very high reputation especially with their "Fruits De Mer" based menu. Running the restaurant was very demanding, particularly during the holiday season, and meant that poor Jack had little or no free time to enjoy family life. Another advantage with Jack's restaurant, was that we had a very pleasant meeting point when it came to discussing business with potential new clients. This also helped Jack whenever he was asked by tourists or potential new buyers where appropriate English speaking help could be found. A facility known in the trade as "wheels within wheels".

By this point in my French adventure, my work was increasingly turning towards translations for house purchase, sales and other legal transactions so I was developing a very useful circle of contacts within the area which helped both myself and the property selling agents. This meant that I could spend more of my working hours in translation work and less in hard labouring work and it was during one of my translation jobs that I met a very charming lady called Genevieve. This lady worked, when I first met her, for a Paimpol based agence immobilier but, because of her long experience in property sales and her language skills, she was in popular demand with other agencies and soon joined a new and quite aggressive agency which opened a shop in Pontrieux. Within a couple of months in Pontrieux, Genevieve's husband bought a small but very popular bar on the river side on the edge of the village and the "networking" intensified to an extent that I began to wonder whether I really wanted my French adventure to take such a sophisticated direction. I had enjoyed, during the early years, learning about the skills involved in building renovation and garden development and had enjoyed a new excitement in discovering my abilities, most of which I had never imagined to be achievable since I had always assumed that, having reached the age of fifty two years, I would have completed my education and could look forward to "coasting along" for the remainder of my working career. The only problem with this voyage of discovery was that the labouring element was becoming more difficult as the years crept by so I decided to "go with the drift" and see where my new direction lead me.

It must be said that I found it much easier being able to convert my new language skills into revenue although I soon realised that the shift in responsibility was, perhaps, not so good. As a young man I had always struggled with what I thought of as "grown ups" and "important people" so, as I became more involved with translations and negotiations, I thought about the irony of clients who I had always classed amongst life's "specials" suddenly depending on little old me to look after their affairs. It has to be said, however, that all of the people I had worked for were perfectly reasonable and remained good friends after my time in France so, perhaps, I had been wrong about my idea of "grownups".

As Winter approached, I found a quiet spell with my work and decided to go back to England for Christmas and the New Year which was likely to be fun since the world was about to celebrate the beginning of the new millennium, it was also going to be Mother's second Christmas back home and I didn't like the idea of her being alone on such a momentous occasion. I was also beginning to realise the importance of being with my daughters and grand children at a time when their families and careers were developing.

When I arrived back home in Pommerit in mid January, I had a call from Derek to meet him at the hotel to discuss his improvement plans and, when I arrived at the bar, there were two English couples already there so I was introduced first to Russell and Louise. They were pleased to tell me that they had just bought the four gites from Richard and David and had decided to come over to live in France to run the gites themselves as a business and, thank you very much, would not need my services there this year! This was not an encouraging start to my new year since I had already lost two gites during the winter with owners who had sold their houses so I had lost forty per cent of my business and had no "new irons" in the fire at that point. The other couple in the bar had been sitting quietly in the corner and were looking as though they wanted to join in with our conversation so I took the liberty of inviting them over and asked them if they were on holiday. They would be best described as being an unusual couple since the husband, John, was of African origin, a rare sight in Brittany, and in his mid forties whilst his attractive wife was very English and somewhat older. They had, apparently, been recently married and had decided to use the money they had gained from the sale of one of their houses to buy a house in Brittany which they could retire to when John's career as a policeman came to an end in five years time. Since I had been working much more, recently, in the property market, I was asked to help them to find a suitable property and was a little surprised to learn that their budget, whilst modest by English standards, was going to put them into a property bracket which I had not been involved in up to that point. Since they were only in France for one week, there was little time to waste so I set off, the following day, on my rounds checking with the local immobiliers and notaires and was immediately impressed by the standard of property that was available within their price range.

By the end of the third day, we found a truly splendid manor house just near to Runan which had been something much more grand than a farm house and had obviously been extended in the past. The entrance, through a stone arched gateway, lead to a courtyard with the main house on the right hand side of the square and extensive stables on the opposite side. The back end of the courtyard had a small building which might, in the past, have been accommodation and a driveway leading off to a farmyard with various ruined barns and the remains of an orchard and ornamental garden. The original manor house had been built on three floors with six bedrooms and a small building on the end housing the remains of a bread oven and cider press. The extension to the main house took the form of an annexe including two more bedrooms and an enormous open barn beyond that. The asking price for the manor was well within the budget and would leave a modest amount of money to begin renovation work inside and restoration work on the garden and surrounding land. The Compromis was signed, deposit paid and completion date agreed for early summer. This was great news for me since it was likely to provide me with enough new work so that, added to the work in Derek's hotel, my lost work on the gites would be more than replaced.

Since several of my client's gites had been advertised in the Brittany Ferries brochure, I was well known to them so it came as a very pleasant surprise when I received their letter inviting me to take up a newly created post as mediator for the gites which they had in their brochure in my area. I quickly realised that this role was not going to earn me a great deal of money but it would look good on my C.V. so I accepted the post and awaited further instructions. By late August of the first season I received my first call asking me to go to a gite some thirty miles away to investigate a complaint received from a family who had rented a gite for two weeks but had to be moved to another gite after two days due to the sorry condition of the gite. I arrived at the gite at the appointed time and checked throughout as instructed. The main complaint was typical of the type of problem which we were accustomed to with tourists who come from "big cities" into the countryside without realising that they have to share the area with lots of "God's little creatures".

It had to be said, however, that those gites with French caretakers tended to be maintained to a different standard to what the English tourists might be accustomed. I needed to be careful in the wording of my report to Brittany Ferries since, for example, the tourists were quite right to complain about the presence of mice in the house but it is common practice, in these houses, to secure all food in sealed containers and not to leave fruit and potatoes sitting on an open shelf overnight. I completed my report and received the appropriate payment for my work but heard no more about the complaint until, some weeks later, all Brittany Ferries registered gite owners were issued with a new set of guidelines on the style and cleanliness of property to be listed as Brittany Ferries approved. I only had that single issue to deal with as a mediator and, two years later, their system was changed and the role of mediator abandoned.

Towards the end of that summer, I was introduced to an English couple who had bought an old shop in the centre of Pontrieux with the ambition of making it into a Bed and Breakfast house and, since it was opposite the only hotel in the village, it seemed to be a good idea. They had, evidently, moved to France to begin their new lives together and Mike, something of a handy man, had visualised the possibility of creating four double bedrooms upstairs with accommodation for himself and Susan on the third floor whilst the large garage had room for his tools and equipment. The ground floor and old shop was converted into a dining area which, they thought, could be used as a restaurant during the day although since the hotel opposite already did the "Menu Ouvrier" they were under no illusions about great revenue from the restaurant. Their next ambition was to try to set up an internet website and Mike begged my old computer in the hopes that he could make it work well enough to set up the website. This worked but, with the condition of the computer, only on Thursday mornings when there was an "R" in the month, if you get my meaning.

It had become apparent that no two summer seasons were the same in terms of numbers of tourists and the year 2000 was not as busy as the previous year so my new friends with the four gites at Pommerit Le Vicomte had not enjoyed the level of business that they had expected. Things were not helped by the fact that they were, themselves, living in the biggest of the gites and had obviously forfeited more than 25% of their potential revenue. Their summer was made more difficult by virtue of the fact that, since they were living on site, the tourists were always around and tended to spend most of their time either making a lot of noise or banging on Russell and Louise's door to ask for help, that, at least, was how Russell and Louise saw the problem.

The other side of the argument was that if you had paid a lot of money to rent a gite, you expected everything to work and to be able to enjoy the facilities including the swimming pool opposite the front door. The decision was taken, by Russell and Louise, to move off site and so they bought a small house on the opposite side of Pommerit so that they could have some privacy whilst still being close to their gites and the hope was that the extra revenue from the fourth gite would help pay for the complete renovation needed in their new acquisition.

It is often tempting, on my part, to try to point out the folly of such business decisions but if one has no such previous experience and "outsiders" are not asked for advice, then mistakes are bound to occur. On the positive side, their new house had a very important neighbour who would soon take a special role in their lives and a greater role in my own life.

The neighbour was a local character who responded to the name of "TiTi", much to the amusement of his new English friends. Evidently, TiTi, like many other people, had acquired his unusual name by virtue of his younger brother's inability to pronounce his proper name and one wondered if this might have influenced his personality since he might have been described as being a little on the unusual side. Being a true Breton, he was quite small in stature, being no taller than me and probably in his early sixties although he had been retired from work for some years due to a work injury which had rendered one of his hands unusable. He had worked, for most of his life, as a builder and was therefore very experienced at building in stone as well as modern materials and so he normally worked in the traditional manner with little more than a trowel, plumb bob and string. One of the many benefits of working with TiTi was that, since he had always worked in the "old fashioned" way, he paid little attention to modern Health and Safety methods and would not be too distracted by working on a site with no access to such luxuries as electricity, safety wear, etc. Nevertheless, his standard of work was very high and one could always have confidence in the end result although, since he was officially retired, he was only allowed to act on a consultancy basis unless, that is, no-one was looking!

As a neighbour to Russell and Louise, he was able to save them a great deal of expense in renovating their newly purchased house whilst teaching Russell to do work that he would never, otherwise, have been able to undertake so that Russell was not only saving money but also learning new skills in the same way that I had when working with Bob the builder some years earlier. With our friend Sven and his digger and TiTi to help Russell and Louise with their renovation, it wasn't long before they had their sceptic tank installed, plumbing and wiring done and a new kitchen fitted so liberating their fourth gite which also helped restore their income. It also helped to have a "tame" builder in my circle of contacts.

Work had already started on Derek's hotel renovation and he had decided that each of his six available letting rooms should have its own bathroom so Derek had a local plumber to install the first fix plumbing while he tackled the electrical installations and wiring himself which meant that I only had to fit the internal tongue and groove cladding to the walls and ceilings to hide the original walls as well as the plumbing and wiring. This work took longer than anticipated since Derek was usually "hanging around" and served more as a hindrance with his not infrequent changes of plan although this was not too serious a problem to me as I was being paid by the hour.

CHAPTER THIRTEEN

Time For Another Change

At the end of my second season living alone in Paradise, I had achieved all I could with my house and had enjoyed my time there but, unfortunately, it is not in my nature to sit still for too long and so I started to think about looking around for a change of location. Life in Paradise was very relaxing but, being on a roadside with fields opposite, woods behind, no views and almost constant dampness around the house, I was beginning to feel almost trapped indoors. The problem was that my work in the property sales business suggested that the supply of cheap properties for renovation in my area was running low and, as the area grew ever more popular as a tourist region, the price of houses was beginning to soar. This I discovered with my first house at Quemper Guezennec which I bought for less than eight thousand pounds and sold six years later for twenty thousand. I was even more surprised when it was sold that Summer for sixty two thousand pounds !!

I had noticed, however, that there was a "land for sale" sign laying in a ditch and almost buried in weeds, on a stretch of road between Quemper Guezennec and Pontireux and was pleased to see it described as "Terrain A Batir" (building land). The land was around half an acre in size and sat on a stretch of road which offered beautiful views across the river Leff valley and just two hundred yards from the river Trieux. I went to the office of the Notaire handling the sale to ask why it had not been sold in the three years since I first noticed the sign and was told that nobody had enquired about it! It was that simple, nobody had enquired about it!

I had known the Notaire for some years and had bought my first house from him so I knew that I could trust his honesty and, therefore, offered his client six thousand pounds for the land and my offer was accepted!!
I couldn't believe my luck, a half acre site with permission to build one house, half a mile from Pontireux, with beautiful valley views and only two hundred yards from a private mooring with bar, restaurant and a small commune owned camp site all for six thousand pounds. I thought about it over night and, the following day, put my house in Paradise on the market having been advised by a local Agence Immobilier that it should be worth over thirty thousand pounds. Within the first two weeks, I was approached by six other immobiliers each offering to sell my house for me and since, under French law, it is the purchaser who pays both Immobilier and Notaire fees, I agreed in the hopes that a rapid sale could be achieved. I waited and waited as the days dragged by with almost no interest being shown until, just before Christmas, I received my first offer on the house of sixteen thousand pounds! That was two

thousand less than I had paid for it so I thought for a little while of a polite way to tell them to go away and got back to work. Nothing else happened until Christmas arrived and I had booked to go back to England for six weeks after Christmas so that I could be with Mother to celebrate her eightieth birthday on the eleventh of February. I had a visitor to the house who offered me the price I had paid for the house. It was obvious to me that, if seven agents couldn't produce anything better, then I should accept the offer and move on so we signed contracts and set a completion date for mid February.

I arrived back in England in early January with one month to organise Mother's birthday party and immediately set about contacting family and friends from the past but was shocked to realise how many of Mother's earlier friends were no longer with us. Fortunately, my parents had always been closely involved with my teenage and motor cycling years so a good number of my old friends were delighted to be invited to celebrate her birthday.

The small commune of pensioner's flats, where Mother lived, included a community room which was available free of charge so we booked her party and my sister set about the task of preparing and organising food and drink. The party was set and guests started to arrive around late afternoon. We had a near perfect mix of nieces and nephews along with some old school friends of mine and some old friends from my motor cycle years including some of my sister's earlier boyfriends. The party was a great success with some of the guests staying until almost midnight. The most important message to emerge was the tremendous respect and admiration that everyone present held for Mother who, through all the trials and tribulations of her long life, had maintained a strong sense of honour and dignity which most modern people might envy. We shall always treasure the memory of that party with the help of the surviving photo's including one of Mother with her daughter, two grand daughters and one great grand daughter.

Since my visit of six weeks was too long to go without any income, I went to a local employment agency to ask if they could offer me any casual work during my stay and was initially pleased to be offered work almost to order. I had, however, not thought to ask what type of work I would be doing so I was inclined to feel a little disillusioned when my first job was for three days only working at a local ladder factory where I was to load lorries in the despatch department. This was followed by two nights of proof reading for a credit card manufacturer and, finally, four weeks work in a telephone call centre. Quite varied, one might say.

Having sold my house in Paradise and having signed a purchase contract on the building plot near to Pontrieux, my thoughts moved towards what would happen when I returned to France later in February. I had determined that my experience and new skills would enable me to build my own house and I had already asked TiTi to help me with the main construction work as well as persuading Sven to dig the foundations and install the septic tank with his digger. My friend Tom was going to help with the water and electricity installation and I should have enough money, from the sale of my house in Paradise, to buy the materials. It all sounded fairly straight forward so I spent my last days in England drawing a plan for my new house which would include all of the better aspects and none of the undesirable aspects which one so often inherits when buying someone else's idea of how to design a house. Plus it would be less prone to dampness than a stone built house and the insulation would be integral instead of being fitted as an afterthought.

I returned to Paradise and then began to realise that there were likely to be some problems and the project might not be as simple as it sounded. My first task was to organise my own living accommodation but I wasn't too concerned since I had two caravans and decided that the larger one would serve as living quarters whilst the smaller one, which I had inherited from my deceased client, could easily be converted into a kitchen protecting me from having to live with too many cooking smells and leaving my living area clear for domestic benefits such as television, etc. The next on my list of must haves was a bathroom although this was helped by my collection of salvaged goods which included a toilet and shower tray with electric shower unit so all I would need to do was build a small shed by the side of the caravans which would also house the water supply, fuse box and fridge freezer. These issues, although not ideal in their design, were minimal compared to my biggest problem of where to put my collection of furniture most of which I was determined not to have to give up. Thankfully, several of my friends offered to store some items and I decided to offer the remainder to the purchasers of the house which they gratefully accepted since, under French law, the value of any extras would be deducted from the value of the house thus reducing purchase fees paid to the Notaire.

Both sale and purchase were completed on the same day, by which time I had organised my move to the extent that I needed only to have my two caravans towed onto my land and arranged in such a way that I could move in as soon as I had built my "bathroom". I was pleased to be helped by the English couple who had bought the bed and breakfast shop in Pontrieux and most grateful to one of my clients whose small gite, on the other side of the valley, was empty for some weeks and had invited me to stay there whilst I completed the move.
The use of his gite was especially appreciated as the weather took a turn for the worst within a couple of days so I was not able to lay the concrete base for the bathroom added to the benefit of using his television and washing machine.

As Easter approached, I was able to move out of Ken's gite in time for his tourists to arrive so I set up my caravans and awning and moved on to my half acre of land. I ordered and received my first delivery of materials and Sven and TiTi arrived to begin creating the footings for my house. I had, of course, had my French architect colleague to convert my envelope back based drawings into a proper design and the village Maire had rubber stamped my application so work could start and we were fairly safe in the knowledge that we would be left alone to get on with the job without the weekly checks normally exercised in other countries. I was impressed from the very start of my project by TiTi's approach to house construction since he had none of the modern laser equipment for measuring, simply lots of string, an old wooden set square, a spirit level and a couple of tape measures. Nevertheless, the base was laid out and measured accurately to within ten millimetres so Sven dug out the footings and dug the floor out to the required depth and an appropriate amount of ready mixed concrete was delivered to provide a base for the foundation blocks. I had chosen to construct my house using concrete building blocks, most common in our area, and TiTi was most emphatic in his accuracy with the first two rows of blocks since, as he pointed out, a ten millimetre discrepancy at the base could grow to ten centimetres by window level and who knows where by roof level!

Once the first foundation blocks were positioned we needed to allow one week for the concrete and cement to cure through so I was free to concentrate on getting my gites and their gardens ready and then to carry on with my work at Derek's restaurant.

With the passing of Easter, my friend with the bed and breakfast in Pontrieux announced that his new project hadn't got off to the start he had hoped for and he would have to try to find some extra work to subsidise his income. I suggested that he might do some garden work for me since my summer work load was becoming so busy that I was having to turn down new work. That, ultimately, was not a good idea although it did mean that my service did not suffer as the spring growth began and I always tried not to lose sight of the help I had received when I first came to live in France.

The summer, once under way, seemed to fly by with every spare minute I had being spent working on my new house. Once the foundations had been put in, the concrete floor was prepared with, to my surprise, a layer of plastic sheet being topped by a six-inch layer of expanded polystyrene. This, I was told, was for thermal insulation and, despite my disbelief, would not be crushed by the six inches of re-enforced concrete about to be put on top of it!!
The day was set, the ready mixed concrete lorry arrived and TiTi, Sven and I braced ourselves for a very hectic half day since the concrete was spread roughly by the lorry and then levelled and smoothed by hand with TiTi up to his knees in wet concrete and Sven and I pushing the surplus with long handled garden rakes. Things, however, started to go wrong after the second delivery of concrete when we were left with an empty space at one end of the house! We will never know whether we had not ordered enough concrete or the supplier had not delivered the amount I had paid for but, either way, we had no option but to rush down to the builder's merchant, buy some sand and cement and mix the final quantity in my concrete mixer.

The final holes were filled in and, just as things started to settle down, the heavens opened and it poured with rain before we could cover the new base so that TiTi's finely finished surface became an uneven base with small puddles. There was nothing we could do so we opened a few bottles of wine and swore politely at whoever had given us such a trying day.

I spent most of my spare time, during the next couple of weeks, tidying my land and Sven came by with his digger to try to level the ground and help create a basis from which I could develop a garden. There was only a two feet high bank between my land and the patch next door but there was a line of small trees by the side of the bank including two plum trees, seven apple trees and two enormous cherry trees in the corner furthest from the road and between the apple trees was a healthy line of bramble so I looked forward to a supply of plums, apples, cherries and blackberries later in the Summer. It seemed easier to put grass seed on the remainder of my land since I already had a ride-on mower with which I could keep my patch looking tidy.

The next, on my list of necessities, was the septic tank and Sven had found me a fibre glass tank which was greatly reduced in price so he turned up with his digger, dug a large hole and dropped the tank in place. With time to spare, he set about digging a three metre wide foundation path running from the road round to the front of my house. All I needed then were two lorry loads of quarry waste, a couple of days hard work spreading the stones and, hey presto, I had a hardcore drive.

It would be untruthful of me to declare that I enjoyed living in a caravan although I was fairly well organised with my small caravan as a kitchen and my bathroom only a few strides away. Besides, it was summer and so I spent most of my time working either in the gites, in the gardens or on my own land. Now, at least I had the new challenge of learning how to build a house and TiTi was freely available to show me how to start building the walls using only a plumb-bob, spirit level and lots of string and, by the time we had completed the third row, he declared that I was safe to carry on alone. There are many aspects of building a house which I had never needed to consider, for example, which comes first, the door or the hole to fit it into? In England, I was told, one supports the door with temporary legs and builds the wall around the door. Whereas, in France, one builds a hole and then fastens the door inside the hole. This meant choosing the door and window frames and creating appropriate spaces as the walls were constructed although one had to hope that the same dimension frames would still be available when the time came to do the fitting. I was assured by TiTi that this had never been a problem in the past and I had no need to worry but, knowing my luck, I wouldn't rest easily until the fitting actually happened.

I carried bravely on and was soon at the height for the window sills so I chose my windows and carefully measured out their relative positions. The only problem with that philosophy was that I couldn't buy my windows since there was nowhere to store them so I had to hope that the same windows were available when the time came to buy them.

As the end of the season approached, Lydia asked me for a chat. She had finished her time at university and had passed her exams and started applying for work so she did not anticipate being able to work with me next year. This was another version of good news and bad news since I was, of course, delighted that she had been successful in her education but naturally disappointed that such a perfect working relationship was coming to an end. Only a few weeks later, she accepted a job as a hostess with Air France on their long haul flights which meant that she would, literally, be flying all around the World. The good news and bad news struck again just a few weeks later when I had a visit from our newly elected village Maire who called on me to see how work on the house was progressing. The bad news was that he wanted me to move my caravans to the ground behind the house so that my site didn't look like a gypsy encampment! Working on my normal philosophy of keeping my head down and my mouth shut, I decided to respect his request and spent the next two days disconnecting, disassembling, moving and re-assembling everything to the new spot only thirty feet away. The most difficult aspect of my move was that the door to my bathroom was now on the opposite side to my caravans so I had to block off the original door and create a new one but with the advantage that I could access my facilities away from the vision of passing cars.

One of the items which I had not budgeted for, after the sale of my house, was my car which had decided to expire on me within two weeks of my move. This was another of those good news and bad news things since I had become dependant on a very tired Renault hatchback which barely coped with carrying my tools whilst towing my trailer with mower so the good news was that, for the first time in years, I was able to afford a new car.

The car sales industry in France seemed, to me, to make little sense as the new cars were cheaper than in England whilst second hand cars were considerably dearer. I drove my old Renault to a local Seat dealer in Guingamp and bought a brand new Seat Ibiza for only six thousand pounds at a time when the same car in England would have cost me seven thousand five hundred pounds! Unfortunately, they would not take my Renault in part exchange so I parked it on my land, out of sight, and used it as a tool store. One great benefit of having a new car was that I could go back to England for Christmas and enjoy the drive without worrying about reliability.

Mother was, as always, delighted to see me when I arrived and even more pleased when I told her that I would be staying for a couple of months. The reason for the longer stay was that, despite the rather stern efforts of my French dentist, my poor teeth were in need of radical attention and I refused to pay the French charges yet again so I needed an English NHS dentist.

In view of my longer stay, I would also need a "proper" job so I applied for one or two and, to my surprise, was immediately accepted by the local motorway service station as a cashier. Not, it has to be said, an exciting prospect but the flexible shift hours would give me daytime hours free, once a dentist had been found. Finding a dentist was almost as easy as finding a job and so work began with fillings and extractions just before Christmas. It was not always easy going in to work whilst sections of my face and mouth were still numb from the anaesthetic and I had some puzzled looks from customers when I drooled and bled whilst trying to smile and chat politely.

When the dental work was finally concluded and the bill was paid, I was not surprised when a neighbour told me that the reason that I had been able to get on to the dentist's list so easily was that he was known locally as the "butcher of Chaddesdon" and people in the know never went there. Never mind, the work was done and I was pleased to be able to smile confidently once more.

My job, at least, was great fun and I enjoyed meeting and chatting with the customers, some of whom were taking a break on long journeys and we even had an occasional French customer so I was able to protect my knowledge of the French language.

I also continued to have free time during the day so I could take Mother out, in my new car, to visit family and friends. Mother did not fully appreciate the car which was, of course, left hand drive and this meant that she, as the passenger, was sitting much closer to oncoming traffic which she found to be a little unnerving.

By mid February, I was ready to take my new car and my new smile back to France so I handed in my notice at the service station, said my goodbyes and set off back to see how my caravans had survived Christmas. I was delighted and relieved to find that everything was as I had left it and none of my tools or equipment had been stolen. Theft was something which hardly ever happened in our area and I was always confident that my two neighbours would have given a measure of protection by their very presence.

My first task was to contact my clients to tell them that I was back in France and ready to tackle any work they needed to have done. To my amazement, three of my clients expressed their surprise at my message since the owner of the bed and breakfast in Pontrieux had told them that I had returned permanently to England and he would be pleased to do their work in the future!! I had offered him some extra work to help him through his difficult first season and this was how he repaid me. Enough said.

It was only a couple of weeks after my return from England when Brittany fell victim to one of its rare spells of severe weather. I awoke, one morning, and was instantly aware of the extreme cold, not unusual in a caravan in mid-winter, but this really was cold and my outdoor thermometer was showing minus seven degrees! I had an electric heater in the caravan so I turned it on and got back into my warm bed to try to motivate myself into starting my new day. By nine o'clock, I had decided that it wasn't going to change so I put on my coat and stepped outside to go to my bathroom in the hope that a hot shower would help. I slid my way through the four inches of snow only to discover that the water was frozen and the shower didn't work so I lit the gas fire in the bathroom and went back to the caravan to do myself a hot coffee whilst I waited for things to thaw out. Another plan failed when I realised that I couldn't light my gas hob because the gas had frozen in the cylinder which was stored outside! By mid-day, things were beginning to improve but I was obviously not going to be able to work as the snow was so severe that driving down Breton lanes, without the benefit of sand or gravel to help clear them, was out of the question. Still, it was nice and quiet with no passing traffic. I spent the rest of the day clearing the snow from my driveway in case the weather improved overnight and was about to begin my evening chores when I received a telephone call from my client with his holiday home just outside the village of Pommerit Le Vicomte where I had built his garden wall. He thought to call to ask if the weather was as bad in Brittany as it was in Doncaster and, if so, could I call round in the morning to check that nothing had frozen.

When I told him how cold it was, he suggested that I should go to the house to check it and stay there until the weather improved so that I didn't die in my caravan and he didn't have to worry about his house. In all of my time in France, there were a few occasions when I was grateful to my better clients for their thoughtfulness and this was, without doubt, one of those times.

It took almost a week for the weather to improve enough for me to go back to the caravan but it wasn't too serious since I had been able to do a good chunk of the work inside Derek's hotel so no time had been lost. When I got myself re-installed in the caravans, I set about drying things out since almost everything was damp including, unfortunately, my computer which refused to concentrate for long enough to enable me to check and respond to my e-mails. I was neither surprised nor disappointed since the computer had served me well and I had been able to copy all of the important information on the computer so nothing serious was lost.

I took myself off to the French version of Currys and had a leisurely look around the computers on offer, most of which were supplied with the latest Windows programme called XP so I selected the machine most appropriate and went home to set it up in the section of my caravan known as "the office". I connected everything to the computer, turned it on and was immediately impressed by the speed and clarity of the new programme until, that was, I tried to connect with the internet.

I am not a computer expert and never will be but, after a couple of hours of trying different possibilities, I came to the conclusion that the main drive of the computer could not see the built in internet modem. I assumed that there must have been a wire off or at least a bad connection and since it was, by then, after seven o'clock in the evening I had to wait until the following day to take it back to the suppliers to ask for a replacement computer.

Since most French businesses and shops closed between twelve noon and two o'clock for lunch, I decided to arrive at the shop at two o'clock and approached the salesman I had seen the day before to explain the problem. It took me half an hour to convince him that I did know where the on/off switch was but he refused to co-operate any further so I carefully explained that I would not leave the shop until I had a satisfactory solution to my problem at which point he took me to the office of the newly appointed lady manageress. She was more than attractive and surprisingly young but just as insistent as the salesman with her challenge to my intelligence so I invited her to turn on the computer and find out for herself. She obliged and enjoyed the same level of success that I had suffered the day before so I suggested that she could simply exchange it for a new one. This, she assured me, was not possible since the computer was now second hand so she telephoned the manufacturer and spent the next two hours following their instructions and re-programming the whole thing.

After two and a half hours, they declared that they would have to send a technician to my home to find and repair the fault but that could not happen until the end of the following week. I took the thing home and spent half of my evening telephoning my clients to explain the problem so that business could be done in the old fashioned way using telephone, pen and paper! The technician arrived on the appointed day and turned my computer on to begin his search for the fault. After ten minutes of asking the hard drive to find the modem, he turned the computer off, removed the outer cover, replaced the missing wire and, hey presto, it worked!! The technician was both embarrassed and apologetic so there was nothing more to be said as he left me to catch up with my lost fortnight of e-mails.

My new season got off to an interesting start when a client, for whom I had done some work to assist in the renovation of his holiday home, called me to ask me to meet him at his house as urgently as possible. I met him there the next day and was a little surprised to see him loading the contents of his house into the back of his van and was even more surprised when he told me that his long standing ambition to emigrate to New Zealand had finally been approved and that he was due to leave in one month!

In view of the tight time schedule, he would need all the help I could offer since the house had to be cleared and made presentable so that it could be sold as soon as a buyer could be found. He had already contacted our "tame" immobilier in Pontireux and was optimistic that someone could be found from, what amounted to, the agent's waiting list. Most successful agencies had a list of prospective buyers who asked to be informed when an appropriate bargain became available and this house certainly fell into that category due to the urgency of the client's situation. It was more than a very pleasant surprise for the client when a buyer was found and compromis signed before he had to return to England for, what would be, the last time.

His final instruction to me was to deal with the final sale, collect the cheque and post it on to him in New Zealand and clear the remaining furniture in the house. My fee for this work would come from any money I could raise from the sale of his furniture which helped me in two ways since I usually had my own list of clients looking to buy rustic style furniture of the type he had left behind, plus there was a fridge/freezer and pine double bed both of which I would need in my own house whenever, if ever, I finished building it.

One aspect of my new residence which also differed from life in a stone house with one metre thick walls was a noticeable closeness to the wildlife with which I was sharing the environment. Thankfully, with the caravans being a foot or more clear of the grass and mud, I only ever had one encounter with mice and, although they did no damage, I quickly dealt with them if only to stop the noise which seemed to be amplified in the pure silence of a night in an open field. One noise over which I had no influence came from a pair of owls which lived nearby. I hadn't previously realised that the normal description of owl song was not "twit twoo" but it was the female who shouted "twit twit" and the male who replied "twoo twoo" so the female would sit on the roof of my car at around two o'clock in the morning and shout "twit twit" to which the male would reply, from the next field whilst I would shout "shut up" (or words to that effect) which neither of them would understand.
There was also a family of wrens, living somewhere in the hedgerow, which accepted me as a friend which was good to have someone to chat to who was only going to sing in reply. They took friendship a little too far, however, if I left a door open they would sneek into the caravan looking, presumably, for something to eat! Fortunately, they would normally heed my invitation not to do anything unpleasant on my computer keyboard.
Despite the fact that I had not had time to begin to prepare a garden, there were sufficient wild flowers around to attract some of nature's vast collection of flying insects including one I had never seen before which would hover in front of the flower and extend its proboscis into the flower by up to one inch. I later discovered that it was called a humming bird tiger moth which is normally seen only in the south of France but had obviously drifted further north due to an unusually warm spell. This array of flying insects attracted a wide range of birds including a skylark as well as several early evening bats. Only two hundred yards away by the river, were the usual collections of egret, heron, moorhen, buzzard and various other birds of prey which made me wish I had learned more about wildlife when at school.

By mid august, I was really beginning to miss Lydia's support, especially on a saturday when I often had to work until ten in the evening but I was always pleased to receive her occasional e-mails with stories of travelling far and wide with Air France. Work, thankfully, continued to find me and included some eccentric characters from all walks of life including, for example, a very pretty young artist from central London. She wanted to buy a house in the countryside to help her creativity and bought a small two bedroomed cottage for half the price of a lock up garage in central London! The cottage was in good condition and needed little work to make it inhabitable so she came over, with her Mother and two men with a van full of flowers, to create a garden. This should have provided me with plenty of maintenance work except that it was around thirty miles from my home so, clearly, she needed and soon found, a local person. Nevertheless, she made a lovely cottage which was soon to become very popular with her London friends.

Towards the end of the season, I had a call from my friend Jack who had been chatting to one of his restaurant clients and had recommended me for some work they needed to have done. An appointment was made for me to meet the client and his wife at their house near to Lezardrieux. Most of the houses I had worked on so far, were pretty but this one was stunning being over one hundred years old, built in stone on a terrace cut into the banks of the river Trieux estuary near to the point where it met the English Channel and enjoyed views both up and down stream.

The house had been extended, some years earlier, giving it four bedrooms with two bathrooms and was fronted by a large patio. The house was built at ninety degrees to the bank so that the kitchen end wall was cut into the bank. The garden ran along the terrace and there was a swimming pool set into the garden. There was a forty-foot drop along one side of the garden down to the river itself. I met a very pleasant gentleman who, I assumed, was the owner but he immediately explained that the house actually had twelve owners who shared the running costs and the house on a time share principle. This, he explained, worked very well except when a problem, such as the current one, arose where the extent of the repair and the projected cost had to be agreed by all of the members or, as he described it, management by committee.

The problem was with a section of the estuary bank which had been cut back to facilitate the patio but was supported by a rather feeble stone retaining wall which had collapsed allowing the section of bank to fall back onto the patio. I was asked to examine the situation, prepare an estimate for the work and report back to him within two weeks by which time he would be back in England and able to discuss it with the other members. It was immediately obvious to me that, being a structural problem, I would need to be sure of the situation before submitting my report so I arranged for TiTi to visit the site with me. This was not going to be an easy problem to rectify and neither TiTi nor I were keen to commit to such a responsibility. Nevertheless, a solution was proposed, a design prepared and a Devis submitted.

We heard nothing for almost one month until I received a call from their spokesman who had come back to France, armed with the committee's summary and I was asked to meet him at the house. He opened our "meeting" with a brief history of the joint ownership of the house describing the members, most of them retired, and their professions. One of the members, it seems, was a retired civil engineer who had looked at our plan and declared that it was over engineered and promptly submitted a much simpler design with his expectation that our Devis should, therefore, be reduced by at least thirty per cent. I showed the design, the next day, to TiTi who was neither pleased nor impressed since his long experience in the building industry gave him to believe that this could not be considered as a long term solution to their problem. Nevertheless, he agreed that we should submit a revised Devis on the understanding that the owners accepted liability for the revised design.

The revised design was approved and work began so Sven arrived with his digger and a small dumper truck so that the rubble could be cleared and the bank was cut back so that the new foundations could be set in readiness for the new wall. Standard concrete blocks were used with re-enforcing rods and a solid concrete infill all of which took a whole week of hard work. We had then been instructed to apply a facing of natural stone tiles with a knee high stone wall in front to provide a flower and shrub border which, it was hoped, would eventually grow high enough to hide the base of the wall whilst ivy and other similar trailing plants were planted along the top of the wall to provide the remaining cover. The stone tile facing was the slowest part of the job since only two rows of tiles could be set then the cement based adhesive had to be left to cure before the next two rows were applied, and so on. After four weeks of work, the finished wall was shown to the owners but, sadly, only the civil engineer was impressed whilst the other owners felt that the overall appearance was "inappropriately modern".

Some weeks later, I was contacted by their spokesman who explained that their cleaning lady had taken time off to have a baby and their gardener had taken his summer holiday so I was asked to trim the garden and clean the swimming pool for a month as well as cleaning the house throughout for their changeovers. This would not, normally, have been a problem except that the first of the visitors was a well known retired B.B.C. reporter so I was unusually nervous but did nothing different in my cleaning prior to his arrival. My heart stopped, on the evening of their arrival, when the person concerned telephoned me to ask who had cleaned the house! I boldly admitted that it was I who had done the work and asked whether there was a problem. My heart restarted when he explained that his wife wanted to thank me for presenting the house in a better condition than their regular cleaner would have prepared it! Phew.

The next visitor also telephoned me but with a different problem. I had been looking after the swimming pool and had noticed that, each time I cleaned the filters, I had to top up the water level in the pool and the latest visitor said that this was not normal and asked if I could arrange for the pool installer to go along and find and repair the leak. He spent half a day ripping up the concrete to expose the pipes and declared that he could find nothing wrong with the plumbing to the pool. He then lowered a flow detector into the pool to check for any uninvited flow of water but could find no obvious leak from the bottom of the pool. He ultimately reported the leak to be higher up in the pool, nearer to the filter return pipe and said that he had put new sealant in place to prevent the problem. Unfortunately, the leak didn't stop and, by the end of the season, the problem became more serious.

My other gite work carried on at an acceptable pace and my work at Derek's hotel had now moved to an extension which he was building at the rear of the hotel. This was a fairly extensive piece of work which involved converting an old Breton style "function" hall into a dining area for weddings and parties and connecting the room to the back of the hotel via a corridor which was to be constructed in concrete blocks with a corrugated roof using the cheapest butyl based sheeting and a series of second hand windows along the side of the corridor. Since finance was, for Derek as for most of us, a critical issue the choice of materials to be used on the project was sometimes questionable but always within the specifications quoted in the building permit.

My surprise came when, one day, Derek asked me whether I would be interested in buying his son's motor bike since his son had passed his driving test and moved into a car so he no longer needed the motor bike. It was only a 50cc motor bike but in a modern style made to look like the next size up so, whilst it looked quite impressive, it was actually quite slow despite being only two years old. The proposition was that I should accept the motor bike as part payment for my labour and that this would save Derek a sizeable sum of cash whilst providing me with a cheap motor bike on which I could "play" on my days off.

I thought about his proposition for a few days and decided that, whilst the bike was not something I would normally have bought, it would give me a hobby toy for my free time and secure my work at the hotel for as long as the payment scheme worked. Furthermore, I would end up with a motor bike which I could sell, perhaps for a small profit, having first enjoyed a little "fun in the sun".

Towards the end of the season, I received another call from the chairman of the house in Lezardrieux. This call concerned their leaking swimming pool which was becoming progressively worse and their civil engineering member had determined that the unprotected section of their land was being slowly eroded by the river causing the garden and therefore the swimming pool to become unstable to the extent that a crack had appeared in the base of the pool causing it to leak. The section of the bank nearest to the house had been stabilised some years earlier by a sea defence specialist contractor who had built a massive supporting wall using five ton blocks of granite rock and this had worked although I couldn't imagine how they had lifted the blocks into place from the river edge.

I was now asked to try to find the contractor to get a devis for the blocking of the remaining exposed bank and was given the only clue available of a single telephone number to enable me to find the contractor. This, surely, had to be my toughest challenge to date but I could not allow my fear to be exposed to the client. After a soothing glass of wine, I picked up my telephone and dialled the number. I was not surprised to learn that the contractor had, long since, retired and was grateful to be given another telephone number which led to another and another until I eventually spoke to a major European road construction company with a sea defences division and an appropriate meeting was arranged on site.

This was another of these challenging events where I learned more new French words and a few construction terms that I had never needed before and would hopefully never need again. A couple of weeks later, I received their devis for the work needed and passed it on to the owners in England only to be told, one week later, that the civil engineer felt the expense was not justified. I decided that, at this point in our relationship, it would be better if I didn't subject my professional time to further tangles with the management by committee system and politely suggested that they take a note of my friend Sven's telephone number instead. I wondered if this was my second introduction to the grumpy old man syndrome.

The winter approached and I set about the usual rounding off ceremony by finishing off the unfinished jobs and giving all of the gardens their final tidy up.

I had enjoyed summer and the jolly jaunts on my mini-motor bike although I was consistently disappointed by its lack of performance so I decided to sell it before returning to England for what had become my annual hibernation. The French law, so far as riding motor bikes is concerned, allows fourteen year olds to ride bikes of up to 50cc capacity so I had no trouble finding a buyer for my bike since it looked very sporty and was capable of sixty miles an hour top speed. I placed one newspaper advert and sold it for the asking price, to a French boy whose parents were pleased to encourage him, and actually made a small profit.

I arrived back in England in late november and was pleased to find a job within two weeks although the pay was very low and I would have to work shifts over Christmas and New Year. The work was simple enough, I was cashier at a local petrol station set in a pleasant stretch of countryside just a few miles from Mother's flat where I planned to stay until early march. By Christmas, I had settled in nicely and, as usual, enjoyed meeting customers although there were more regular customers since the station was mid-way between Derby and the village of Melbourne and I did not enjoy working alone especially when on the late shift. I was working alone on New Years

Eve but had been told to close the station at nine thirty so I arranged to go to my daughter's house, straight afterwards, to celebrate the new year. I closed the station just after nine thirty, secured the valuable stock such as the cigarettes and locked the cash in the underfloor safe, as usual. I set the alarm code and locked the door before walking across the forecourt to my car and was just twenty feet or so from the car when I heard a scuffling noise behind me. As I turned to investigate the noise, I was pushed to the ground by the first of three men who had been hiding behind the garage. They were not gentle with me, despite my protestations, and dragged me, by the feet, around to the back of the garage where they tied my hands and feet. Two of the men had sawn-off shotguns and they took the garage keys from me and asked me for the alarm code then they left me with one man pointing his shot gun at my head.

Only a couple of minutes passed by before they were back, in very angry mood, demanding to know the code number for the safe. This was my first taste of true fear because I had no idea of what the code was for the safe and I was probably not very convincing until they took the safety catch off of the gun. At this point, I was in fear of my life and could only hope that they would accept my explanation. It was probably only ten minutes, but it felt like an hour, before they were back, bags full of cigarettes and pockets bulging with what I assumed to be money. They then asked me where I lived and assured me that, if they were caught by the police, they would see that I paid the price.

At that point, they jumped over the fence behind the garage and ran off across the adjoining field leaving me, still on the floor and tied hand and foot. There was silence and I was alone and alive and, I am not ashamed to confess, crying but sufficiently alert to try to unbind my hands and feet so that I could go round into the garage and telephone the police. By the time the first police car arrived, I was in a state of shock and trembling almost uncontrollably so that the first policeman took me into his arms to try to comfort me and reassured me by pointing out that God was, obviously, not ready for me! By the time the second car arrived, the police helicopter was overhead and scanning the nearby fields and lanes. A whole hour passed before I was able to telephone my daughter to tell her what had happened and the police reassured me further by telling me that they had already sent a car to Mother's flat and would wait with her until I was able to go home. The garage owners finally arrived by which time I was in a fit condition to drive to Mother's flat but with a police escort. I was immediately asked to give my jacket and trousers to the police in case they had evidence on them and my final instruction was to go to the relevant police station as soon as I could, the following day. We arrived, mid-morning, and made and signed our respective statements after which, the police photographer carefully photographed my cuts and bruises and we were assured that most of the robbery had been filmed on the CCTV both inside and outside of the garage.

By the time we arrived back at Mother's flat, the effects of the robbery were beginning to make themselves felt and I began to feel quite ill. Try as she might, Mother could not help and things did not improve when the police arrived to install a temporary panic button. This, they assured us, was connected directly to the police station so that we could send for help if we thought that we were under any kind of threat from the robbers.

By mid-afternoon, both of my daughters had arrived and were as traumatised as Mother but with sufficient sense of logic to determine that I needed some form of medical help. Unfortunately, since it was New Year's Day, nothing could be done so I stayed in the flat until the doctor could be consulted. It took the doctor only a very little time to determine that I was suffering from post traumatic stress disorder and I was immediately referred to an appropriate therapist.

I am constantly aware that there are a great many people who have, like me, survived life threatening experiences and yet each one is an individual event as are their consequences and so life, for me, could never be the same again.
The initial therapy was likely to take a couple of months so I had to try to find other employment and considered myself to be fortunate to be offered another cashier job this time at the local airport. My employer was sympathetic to my problem and allowed me time away from work to visit my therapist.

My eldest daughter had suggested I contact a "no win, no fee" solicitor to investigate the possibility of claiming against the garage owner for compensation. A very efficient and somewhat aggressive solicitor was found who immediately started work on my behalf. He explained that my first approach would be to the garage owner who would, no doubt, be insured. This was likely to produce our best result but there was also a government scheme which, although much slower, might help if successful. He also suggested that my Mother might have a case although, as my next of kin and not a direct victim, any compensation would be much less.

As my therapy programme approached its closing stages and my treatment sessions almost completed, I still found myself unable to go out after dark as one of the side effects of my condition was my response to unidentified noises which sometimes caused very unpleasant panic attacks.

By the end of february, I was beginning to feel a little better so I decided to go back to France where I could, at least, relax a little. My building plot had only one immediate neighbour so I would be less likely to suffer panic attacks. I had plenty of gardening work and a couple of minor works to do on other gites as well as my own project which was progressing slowly since I was having to move and lift all of the blocks and cement by myself. I decided that it would ease my concern about unidentified noises and panic attacks if I fitted a couple of floodlights outside especially after experiencing one of these attacks when an apple fell out of a tree as I was walking back to my caravan one dark night. The plan worked although my neighbour wasn't too impressed with my constantly lighting up his garden as well as mine.

My summer season was, thankfully, off to a smooth start since I had, as usual, replaced lost clients with new ones and I had no peculiar problems to face as I had suffered the previous year. This also meant that I was able to carry on with my work at Derek's hotel which was making slow but steady progress.

With most of my friends, from my earlier years in France, having moved away my social life was somewhat diminished although my client, whose motor bike I had ridden, continued to provide me with occasional work rewarded by a most enjoyable series of parties and barbecues where I was able to help with translation between English and French guests. Having sold his motor bike the previous year, Andrew had decided to buy a small boat so that his wife and children could join him on his little outings.

He bought himself a rigid inflatable boat with a small outboard motor which was ideally suited to excursions along the river. It was not, however, in Andrew's nature to settle for something as modest as an inflatable boat so, at the end of the season, he decided to sell it and invited his neighbour's daughter and myself to join him on his last trip out and to help him to load the boat onto its trailer so that he could return it to the boatyard from where he had bought it. This was the first and only time that I had piloted an inflatable boat which was quite different to the larger boat that my daughter and I had enjoyed on our trip to the Isle De Brehat some years earlier. I quickly realised why Andrew wanted a larger boat and was inclined to agree with his revised ambition.

As autumn passed and winter approached, I was starting to plan my Christmas in England and my schedule was brought forward when I received the news that my solicitor had been successful with my compensation claim for the robbery. I rushed back to England and was delighted to collect a cheque which repaid me for my lost earnings since the robbery and left me with sufficient money to buy the remaining materials I needed to finish the building of my house. This was especially good news since I was already one year behind schedule and life, in a field, in a caravan, with post traumatic stress disorder was almost impossible so I determined to cut short my English Winter so that I could get on with my house project. In the meantime, I was looking forward to Christmas and had been fortunate to find a few weeks agency work in a warehouse which was far from exciting but reasonably well paid and not stressful, all of which helped my traumatic condition.

Having received my initial claim settlement from my solicitor, we then discussed Mother's claim which was likely to take longer to realise and was, if successful, going to be for a much smaller amount. Nevertheless, he was determined to pursue the claim starting with the garage insurance company but, within a couple of weeks and before my return to France, we were assured that no responsibility was going to be accepted and the claim was rejected. The next step, he declared, was to pursue a government scheme which was much more modest in its amount and would take much longer to achieve but, nevertheless, worth while.

With our immediate compensation claims dealt with and Christmas spent in much more cheerful spirit than the previous year, I was keen to get back to France so that I could get on with my house build. As soon as my agency job ended, I rushed back to France and purchased all of the materials I would need to complete the formal structure with the final purchase to include the windows and doors. I was not surprised to learn that the door and window sizes had changed but the new dimensions would not affect the finished product so work carried on and I was looking forward to getting back on schedule with my project.

My summer season got off to an early start and I was introduced to two new clients who had bought houses nearby and were looking forward to experiencing "La Vie En France" on a regular basis whilst renting their houses, through an agency, when they were not using them for their own holidays. The houses were quite different from each other, with one house being a large town house in the centre of a small village whereas the other one was a small manor house built on the top of the Trieux valley. The town house was built on three floors and had four bedrooms and two bathrooms but no off street parking and a very small garden just big enough for a family barbecue. The only "complaint" I ever received was that the owners had refused to provide a television which, given the occasional inclement weather, was very necessary.

The other house also had three floors, four bedrooms and two bathrooms but had an additional "Granny flat" and a beautiful garden of around three quarters of an acre with Fig and Walnut trees. The subtle difference which I had noticed was that my clientele was increasingly comprising people who seemed more concerned with the investment value of their properties, almost as though they were intentionally moving their money out of England. I began to wonder whether my imagination was becoming overactive or could there be some changes developing within the traditional English financial system?

CHAPTER FOURTEEN

An Unexpected Disaster

Once I received my delivery of building materials, I was able to continue building and was at top of window level when my friend TiTi came to review my progress and declared that I was ready for my ring beam. This, he assured me, was necessary to provide support over the top of the windows and doors, to create a holding frame for the walls and to provide a solid base for the first floor beams which would support the bedroom flooring.

We set about the task of forming a wooden shuttering around the entire building and placed steel re-enforcing frames into the shuttering ready for the concrete which would then complete our ring beam. Once the first mix of concrete was poured into the shuttering, we couldn't stop until the complete ring was filled since, if we did stop and the first mix started to cure, a weak spot would occur once the final mix was poured in. There followed several hours of very hard work with me mixing the cement and passing it up to TiTi and, by dark, we were very tired with several aches and pains in places where we didn't know that we had muscles!
The pain didn't subside until we finished our second bottle of wine which made the start of the following day somewhat difficult. Nevertheless, when I dismantled the shuttering two days later, I had a substantial ring beam and the building was beginning to look like a house.

My gite work was going quite well until mid-august when I was preparing for a day of cutting grass. As I pushed my mower up the ramps and on to my trailer, one of the wheels slipped off of the ramp and the rear of the mower hit me squarely in the stomach causing me a pain so harsh that I knew instinctively that some serious damage had occurred. Unfortunately, when you live alone in the countryside, it makes no difference when you shout for help so I sat on the back of the trailer and smoked a couple of cigarettes until the pain began to subside enough for me to get back to my caravan.

I decided to spend the rest of the day working on my computer and hoping that whatever had happened to my stomach was not going to take long to clear up and that I would be able to carry on with my work the next day. I was just about able to work the following day although any attempts to lift my mower caused me considerable discomfort so the two days of work actually took me one week to complete.

It was one of those events which one knows, instinctively, is serious so I decided that

I would not tell Mother when I telephoned her, as I did on a daily basis, because there would be nothing that she could do but to worry. I was also unable to carry on with my house building, because of being unable to lift above head height, so progress in every direction was virtually frozen and I became somewhat depressed as well as being worried.

Help eventually arrived when one of my clients came over to France with her own team of builders who were going to convert one of her outbuildings into another gite. The team was comprised of two brothers, one a bricklayer and the other a joiner, plus a labourer so I kept my eye on their working skills and rate of progress in case there was a chance of them helping me when they had finished their conversion.

They were quite efficient and their quality of work left little to be desired so I discussed, with my client, the possibility of them being able to help once they had finished the conversion. They came to visit my site and were enthusiastic about getting involved with the building and suggested that it wouldn't take many days to achieve the next phase so a price was negotiated and I looked forward to their arrival on site the following week.

All of the work I had done, so far, had been either with Sven or TiTi and both of them were accustomed to working at the standard French pace of "working until you had had enough". This English team, however, were quite different and obviously used to the English system of starting early and getting "stuck in" until the job was finished so that, by Friday lunch time, the next phase of my project was complete. I was both impressed and delighted because I now had a structure with its walls built, including gable ends, and roof timbers on including two dormer style windows on the back side of the roof.

I was especially pleased with the dormer windows because the planning authorities had objected to them reasoning that such windows were meant to be south facing but my house was built in such a way that the views over the river valley were to the north of the house whilst the south face of the house was facing the road.

With my dormer and patio windows facing north, across the valley, I would enjoy beautiful views whilst protecting my privacy from the inquisitive eyes of passers by. The house was really beginning to take shape and one no longer needed an imagination to realise how beautiful it was going to be.

During the mid-summer period, I became aware of an English car which was regularly parked on the roadside, which ran parallel to the river, between Pontrieux and my house so I took the liberty of stopping there to say hello to the owners of the car. The husband was a very quiet man, almost antisocial one might say, whilst the wife was a much more robust person, both physically and socially, and I was immediately made welcome and invited to look around their newly acquired retirement home. They had, apparently, been running a successful little pub in the south west of England and had sold it to enjoy an early retirement in France and so had rented a house in nearby Paimpol whilst they looked around locally for a house by a river.

The house was quite big enough for them with a very pleasant garden and had its own mooring for a boat immediately across the road. The husband, Richard's, idea of retirement was to enjoy a late breakfast and to take a gentle stroll into Pontrieux before walking back, stopping in all the bars en route, to arrive home in time for a late lunch. Most of this could be done with no better command of the French language than "Un verre de vin rouge s'il vous plait". His wife, Judith, was quite different and most impressively energetic spending hours re-organising the garden, re-decorating the house and sending e-mail messages to all of her family and friends from "her previous life". We quickly became good friends and I would often call in to share a glass of wine with them on my way home.
By late summer, Judith had done all she needed in their house and garden so I asked her if she would like to help me, occasionally, with my cleaning work in the gites since my stomach problem was getting worse and I was not able to operate as efficiently as in previous years plus my translation work was taking more of my time. Thus began a professional relationship which bode well for the future.

At the same time, I was introduced, by an existing client, to a new client with a very complex problem who needed my translation skills. He and his wife had bought a building plot near to Brest and had designed their dream retirement home which, they anticipated, would take two years to complete and would be ready in time for them to enjoy their latter years near to the west coast of Brittany.

The project was going well with the foundations, cave and underground car park built and ready for the house itself to be constructed when, tragically, the client's wife died. During the poor lady's final illness, she had asked him to promise that he would finish the project so that he could enjoy the house in his retirement and perhaps re-marry. Understandably, he had no enthusiasm for the project in its original form since it would have been too large and "full of sad memories".
I was asked, therefore, to help him to re-negotiate the building permit and to arrange for the architect and the building contractor to modify the design to complete the house on a more modest scale. My role, in the revised project, was somewhat tedious since the French bureaucracy is at least as complex as in England and the building contractor was not keen to proceed with the revised design since the structural stresses would be different to those for which the foundations had been designed. The task was made more difficult as the site was around eighty miles from my home so every meeting took the best part of the day. By the end of that summer, a basic revision had been jointly negotiated and the plan was for work to continue the following spring

until, that is, the client found some problems with the design and construction of the existing foundations and we were back to square one!

During the early part of that summer, one of my more long standing clients had decided to buy a second house to renovate and rent out. He had chosen another town house, again with no land, in a very pretty village near to the old merchant town of Treguier. This house was a traditional house, on three floors, with a large living area with kitchen on the ground floor, two bedrooms on the first floor and a large attic in the roof space. My client, being a design engineer, decided that he could fit five bedrooms and three bathrooms into the area on the two upper floors along with a kitchen, dining area and washroom on the ground floor! This was, clearly, going to test my building skills to a new level since the creation of so many rooms in such a confined area would mean inch perfect measurement. This meant that we had to use the thinnest plasterboard available, for the internal walls so that the bathroom furniture would fit in the space allowed! My learning curve, apparently, was to continue.

As winter approached, I made my plans to hibernate and booked my ferry back to England but decided before returning to have the roof slated on my house so that I wouldn't have to worry about the effects of the winter weather on the exposed roof timbers. My friend TiTi had some friends who were willing to do the work and they declared that it would take them three days, provided that I paid them in cash, so a price was agreed and they arrived one Friday morning and were finished by Sunday evening! Hey Presto!! My beautiful house now needed only the patio doors and I could begin to construct the internal walls so, by the time I went back to England for Christmas, my dream was beginning to come to fruition.

The problem was that my stomach condition was getting worse and I realised that my first task in England was to visit a doctor to find out what was wrong. Having been out of England for some time, I had to hope that my last doctor still had my records and would agree to see me so it helped that we had been members of the same club before I moved to France. It was good to see my old friend, after so many years, but the news was not so good since he gave me a fairly thorough examination and declared that I most probably had a hiatus hernia, adding that I would need to avoid any heavy lifting since that would make it worse! This was more than bad news since half of my work in France involved heavy lifting and that included building my house! I went back to Mother's flat and gave her the bad news, what was I to do now?

Things didn't get any better when Mother received a letter from our solicitor saying that her claim for compensation, after the robbery, had been rejected and, although we have a right to appeal, he didn't feel that he would be able to pursue the claim any further. With the robbery and its effect during the previous winter and now the failure of Mother's claim and the news of my hernia, we were both as depressed as we could be and close to despair. Nevertheless, Christmas was fast approaching and we needed to cheer ourselves up and turn negative into positive. I decided that, with or without the solicitor, I would appeal to the government appeal board since Mother had always been honest and did not deserve to be swept aside by a panel of judges who knew nothing about her. Besides which, her fear of "what might happen" had made her become almost agoraphobic and, therefore, housebound.

It was soon after Christmas when I received a letter from the appeals panel inviting me to appear before them in a couple of weeks time, that was the good news. The bad news was that I had to go to an office in central Birmingham so I had to go by train from Derby armed with all of the paperwork I could find including a report from Mother's doctor. I was worse than nervous by the time I arrived in central Birmingham, especially having to battle my way through crowds of people and was close to a panic attack as I sat in the waiting area.

Fortunately, I had calmed down by the time that I was called into the hearing but found the environment somewhat intimidating as I sat, alone, before the members of the panel. The meeting lasted just over half an hour, although it seemed like two hours, and I was asked to wait in a private room whilst they deliberated. I was invited to join them, some time later, and had difficulty in concealing my emotions as they told me that they had decided to accept my appeal and would award the appropriate fee to Mother! The train journey back to Derby passed in a haze of excitement and Mother's relief, when I told her the news, brought tears to our eyes so the whole event, stressful though it was, had been worthwhile. Needless to say, our solicitor had difficulty in making a sensible reply when I telephoned him with my news.

Having reached a seriously low point on the run up to Christmas, things were improving by the end of January when my daughter introduced me to a friend of hers and her husband. They had recently bought a small camp site in the Vendee region of France and wanted to know if I could go there for a couple of months in June and July to prepare the caravans and tents so that it would be ready for them to operate when they arrived there themselves when the school term ended. This sounded like an interesting new challenge for me since I would have time to get my own gites ready for the season and would be back in time for my own busy period in Brittany so we agreed my fee and shook hands on our arrangement.

I packed my bags and sailed back to my new house in good time so that I could get the usual garden preparations done along with the painting and other general maintenance work.
My client, whose boat had been sold at the end of the previous summer, arrived for his Easter break and was pleased to show us his latest acquisition, it was moored up at the marina in Lezardrieux. He had bought a beautiful new boat at the London Boat Show and it was an absolutely stunning craft as you would expect considering it cost a quarter of a million pounds! It looked more like a yacht than a boat, to me, with a

main deck with bar, a control deck above and three bedrooms with two bathrooms below deck with more fixtures and fittings in the kitchen than in an average house. He was most keen to start using it and had set up a website to promote days out and fishing trips for businessmen and tourists. He had studied and qualified for the necessary licence and we were pleased to join him on his first major outing on a trip round the Isle De Brehat.

The passage out of the river Trieux was superb but the open sea was a little choppy as we took to the north side of Brehat but we never had any concerns since he and his magnificent boat coped well with the conditions and the passage between the island and the mainland was both smooth and relaxing.
We were most impressed with his new boat and were suitably disappointed for my client when he discovered a leak on the pipe joining the two toilets which had dumped some horrible smelling substances into the section of the hull which could only be accessed by the manufacturers!

My season's preparation was helped very considerably by my new friend Judith who was doing a superb job with cleaning, vital for arriving tourists, as well as helping me with some of the gardening. I had, therefore, no worries about leaving my work for her to look after when the time came for me to go to the Vendee to prepare the camp site.

I packed some clothes, some tools and my portable television and set off on a journey which took me the better part of the day which was not bad considering I didn't have satellite navigation.

I was most surprised, when I arrived, to discover that the camp site, where I was intended to work, was only a section of a much larger camp site which was divided and shared between four other small independent companies along with the main section belonging to the site owners. I spent most of the first day exploring the site which was very well laid out with a bar, café and shop by the entrance along with a fair sized swimming pool. There were several sections to the site, each surrounded by a shoulder high hedge, which were reserved for tents and set immediately behind the bar and pool. The remainder of the site was neatly set out with, I estimated, over one hundred mobile homes.

The centre of the site was kept clear for touring caravans and tents, all with power supplies and each section with its own toilet and shower block so that the whole site presented an impressive image to the visitors. Since I enjoyed a good command of the French language, I had no difficulty in finding the equipment I needed for the tents which I had to erect and in quickly getting to learn about the way that the camp operated so no time was lost in my preparations. My employer had ten tent sites and a further six mobile homes each with two bedrooms and I had been invited to stay in one of them during my stay. The mobile homes were both attractive and very comfortable with bedrooms at each end and a kitchen/dining area, with bathroom off, in the centre so I was able to set up my television in the central area and soon had my portable satellite dish pointing in the right direction.

Since I had arrived in June, there were very few holiday makers on the site so the evenings were fairly quiet which, with the warm weather, made it feel more like a paid holiday. The area of the site devoted to tents comprised of four areas each run by a franchise, like that of my employer, and the on-site agents for these companies worked very well together each helping the other when needed so I didn't have to worry too much with heavy lifting as help was always available. My situation was made easier by virtue of being the only person in the group who spoke French properly so I was often asked to translate.

There was a small town nearby with the charming name of St.Gilles Croix De Vie where there were a couple of supermarkets and many gift shops, bars and cafes along the main street which lined the beach. I eventually found an internet café which meant that I could communicate with Judith and the rest of my clients. Unfortunately, the French internet service, at that time, was best described as inadequate so there were days when I was not able to contact the outside world but there was a very efficient telephone card system so that I could, at least, telephone Mother on alternate days.

The region, generally, was very pretty and typically clean with various museums, fun parks and the likes interspersed with innumerable camp sites and caravan parks making it an ideal holiday destination for visitors from all around Europe. Although I felt that, since the area was quite flat, it had none of the scenic beauty of my beloved Brittany.

The European element of the camp site, where I was based, meant that there were two English owned franchises as well as two Dutch and one German so we had fun comparing the various company rules and other cultural differences. I especially enjoyed meeting my fellow English agent who, like me, had never experienced this type of work before. This girl had been employed to set up and look after several tents and mobile homes but, with no previous experience and less back-up, was forever asking me questions for which I had no answer. A condition known in the trade as the blind leading the blind.

Having only recently bought the franchise, my employer had the added difficulty of finding the necessary equipment for the tents which appeared to have been abandoned, by the previous owner, in various outbuildings on two camp sites. One of them was around five miles away so I lost a lot of time trying to find the various pieces of my jig saw before I could begin to assemble it. Since I had never had to erect a tent before, this was not going to be easy. Just to help things along, we had a couple of weeks of very hot weather with temperatures in the high thirties which, with my stomach condition worsening by the week, meant that my tent erection work took twice as long as it should have.

Nevertheless, everything was ready in time for the first tourists and I was able to enjoy the social element of life in the Vendee and meeting the site owner's staff as they gathered in readiness for the rush. As the tourists began to arrive in July, the atmosphere changed and it became necessary to lock up and secure tools and equipment especially after my Australian fellow agent had her bicycle stolen. This was a disaster for her since it was her only transport and her English employer refused to replace the bike. So we found a shop in St.Gilles Croix De Vie which sold second hand bikes and were fortunate to negotiate a fair price for a replacement after which event, she referred to me as her "knight in shining armour".

As the end of July approached and my work was almost complete, my English employer called me to say that he would arrive the following weekend to run the franchise himself. So my fellow agents very kindly organised a barbecue to say goodbye after which, I packed my belongings and set off home. I drove back to Brittany reflecting on my eight week adventure, new friends and the thought that I could now add "tent erector" to my C.V.

As I drove towards Guingamp and turned off of the route nationale, I realised that I would be happy to spend the rest of my days in the Cotes D'Armor region of France with its beautiful scenery and gorgeous beaches. For the first time in many years, felt that I might be establishing my roots which Dudley had told me about so long ago.

I arrived at my home and unpacked, having first had a quick check to see that everything was as I had left it and then went down towards Pontrieux to see Judith and Richard. They had coped perfectly well in my absence so we had our de-briefing over a glass or two of red wine. I went back home and spent the rest of my evening sending e-mails and telephoning clients so that I would be able to get back to normal in time for our short but hectic summer season.

By the time I had caught up with my grass cutting, however, my stomach problem was getting much worse and the pain and discomfort had become almost constant. I was beginning to worry especially since my Father had died of cancer at the age of fifty eight and I was now fifty eight years old. I battled and worried my way through August when I reached the point of vomiting stomach acid. I began to panic. My beautiful dream had gone slowly down hill over the last year and so I determined that my illness had to be treated and that would have to happen in England where health treatment was "free" and my Mother and daughters were nearby if I needed help. I spent many hours in deep thought and finally came to the conclusion that my great adventure was over and that I would have to sell my house and return to England where I could spend however much time was available to me with my family and friends. There was an internet website, based in Brittany, specifically for English residents, owners and tourists so I placed an advert for my part-finished house and set the price at less than half of its market value, when finished. Within four weeks, a buyer was found and a sale agreed so I arranged to store my furniture in the garages and attics of friends and prepared to return to England.

There are no words to adequately describe my emotions during this time since my French adventure had been an experience which I could never have imagined. Although difficult at times, I would always hold fond memories of my fourteen years in France, helped by the collection of hundreds of photographs which I had accumulated.

Having decided to go back to England, I had to inform all of my clients and, of course, my friends Judith and Richard who were sorry to receive my news but happy to take over my gite work. Most of my other work was either completed, as usual at the end of the summer, or passed on to my various contracting friends. Needless to say, whilst my Mother and daughters were worried about my health, they were delighted to know that I would be with them to enjoy family life and to get to know my grandchildren. So far as my friends in Brittany were concerned, I had decided that it was better for me not to say too much so that my departure could be quick and clean.

This was a very difficult time for me, as I arrived back in England, so my first task was to register with the local doctor and ask him for his help and then to try to find somewhere to live. The doctor was very helpful and understanding, he even understood my concern about reaching the same age as my Father since his Father had been through the same phase in his life.

He immediately referred me to the local hospital and I was subjected to endless tests which involved having cameras inserted into places where cameras never intended to go. It proved to be worthwhile since, by Christmas, they had determined that I didn't have cancer although the list of problems which I did have, and the damage that had occurred, meant that I would have to take tablets for the rest of my life. This came to me as good news although it was not the way I had wanted my adventure to end.

Finding somewhere to live turned out to be the least of my problems, thanks to an extremely helpful local council, and I was lucky enough to find employment within a couple of months. I enjoyed Christmas and paid my last visit to Brittany to complete the sale of my house. Everything went well until I came to transfer my house sale money from my French bank to my English bank account since the French bank sent my money to Belgium instead of England and it took two months to find it.

Perhaps, I thought, this was France's final goodbye.

Windmill

Derek's
place

Snake

Best horse race

Bob

Emmy full stride

Concrete
foundation

First block

Lez goat

Limoges

Mare and foal

Pointing wall

Ready for roof

Septic tank

Staircase

Downstream

Finished house